THE
INTERNATIONAL STUDENT'S GUIDE
TO THE
AMERICAN UNIVERSITY

D1712937

THE
INTERNATIONAL STUDENT'S GUIDE
TO THE
AMERICAN UNIVERSITY

Gregory A. Barnes
Director of Programs in
English as a Second Language
Drexel University

National Textbook Company
a division of *NTC Publishing Group* • Lincolnwood, Illinois USA

Cover photo:
COURTESY OF NORTHWESTERN UNIVERSITY

Published by VGM Career Horizons, a division of NTC Publishing Group.
© 1991 by NTC Publishing Group, 4255 West Touhy Avenue,
Lincolnwood (Chicago), Illinois 60646-1975 U.S.A.
Library of Congress Catalog Card Number: 90-063850
Manufactured in the United States of America

1 2 3 4 5 6 7 8 9 VP 9 8 7 6 5 4 3 2 1

ACKNOWLEDGMENTS

THIS BOOK BENEFITED FROM THE ADVICE AND SUGGESTIONS OF MANY colleagues. I wish to thank Sandra Barnes, Barbara Hoekje, and Robert Kaplan for reading the manuscript in draft and helping me reshape it. Drexel Admissions officers Keith Brooks and Mary Beth Sowa also read portions of the manuscript and in addition, provided materials for my use, as did Cheng Yan and James Merrick of the International Services Office. Richard Binder of the Drexel University Library cheerfully met all my requests for documents and sources, and Ann Glusker of the University of Pennsylvania Office of International Programs provided a wealth of information on foreign student affairs. Cathrine Berg, James Brownell, and Mary Lee Folcher of the Drexel English Language Center helped me gather quotes from students about the process of becoming a student in the United States; Yumiko Ihara and Motoko Kobayashi assisted by surveying their fellow intensive program students for interesting stories. Various people and institutions provided pictures, for which I have credited them in the captions.

I appreciate also the advice and assistance of Michael Ross and Kathleen Schultz of National Textbook Company.

Drexel University   Gregory A. Barnes

CONTENTS

PART II: THE APPLICATION PROCESS

PART III: ONCE YOU ARE THERE

CHAPTER 1

THE INTERNATIONAL STUDENT IN THE UNITED STATES

One of my friends in the U.S. appreciated my courage to enter this country. She said, "A Chinese lives in America just like an American lives on the moon." But I don't think so, because I make a lot of new friends in the U.S.

—A student from China

NEARLY 14 MILLION STUDENTS ATTEND COLLEGES AND UNIVERSITIES in the United States—14 million men and women, young, middle-aged, and old, from every ethnic background, and indeed, from countries around the world. At least another 14 million men and women from outside of the United States would like to join the group already there. They believe that they will be able to attend an American college or university, and they have reason for their hopes: Their opportunities for study in the United States are very good. Many of them will accomplish their goals if they prepare carefully and—like you, the reader—follow the procedures that are outlined in the following pages.

This book is meant to give you an advantage over millions of other applicants. It is not the only publication you can read about studying in the United States; in fact, many books, articles, guides, and brochures are available, and several will be recommended to you here for study. But this one is comprehensive, in that it gathers together the most important points you need to know. In brief, it takes you through three stages, from the process of finding the information you need, through putting together a successful application, to adjusting to the special requirements of an American city, campus, and classroom.

It will also carry you inside American institutions. You will have a look at colleges and universities in the United States so that you

1

Figure 1-1 Stanford University, California *(Courtesy of Stanford University)*

can compare the American system of education with your own. It then provides a "tour" of American agencies and consulates in your country—the places you will need to visit as you work through the application process. Discussion of the various steps in your process will contain advice to you as well as description, because you must learn ways to make your application attractive and your arrival in the United States easy. Within the chapters, each topic begins with a heading, so that you can follow the main ideas easily. You will also read the words of students who have started their own adventure in the United States; their reactions should be helpful.

At the end of the book, a section called "Sources" lists the publications and documents that provided much of the information for this book, and which you may consult on your own.

"College" and "University"

Your first task is to understand certain terms that will be used again and again. The first of these is the word *American*. There are many peoples in North and South America and they all have the right to consider themselves Americans. For convenience' sake, however, the word will refer here to citizens and situations "of the United States," as in "American education." Perhaps Mexicans and Brazilians and Caribbean islanders—and all the other people of the Americas—will forgive this usage.

Several special terms are used in "American" higher education—in the system of higher education in the United States. Thus, this book is directed to those who want to study at "colleges" and "universities" or in "ESL programs" (programs in English as a Second Language). These are different types of third-level or *tertiary* institutions (that is, they are preceded by primary and secondary education). A "university" in the United States, for example, is a tertiary institution of learning that is characterized by

- An emphasis on research as well as teaching

- The awarding of higher degrees—the master's (M.A., M.S., MBA, etc.), the doctorate (Ph.D., M.D., Ed.D., etc.)—as well as baccalaureate degrees such as Bachelor of Arts (B.A.), Bachelor of Engineering (B.E.), Bachelor of Science (B.S.), and Bachelor of Business Administration (B.S.B.A.), among others

- A broad range of disciplines, or fields of study: several fields of business, of engineering, of liberal arts, and so on

If you want to be a post-graduate student (a "graduate student," as Americans call it), you will apply to a university.

If you are an undergraduate student, you may apply to either a college or a university. "College" does not mean the same thing in the United States as it does in Great Britain or in other countries where educational systems follow a European model. It too is a tertiary institution, but typically it offers *only* baccalaureate degrees and *only* in one large area of study such as the liberal arts. There are also two-year colleges, such as community colleges, which award *associates' degrees* (A.A.).

One more academic term should be defined before we continue: The word *faculty* in the United States does *not* mean a department, or group of departments, as it does in British English. It refers to the entire group of people teaching at the university. Thus, whenever this book uses the words *faculty* or *faculty members*, it means people—the professors and others who do the teaching. What Americans call a group of departments (in business, engineering, etc.) is a college. Thus, there are colleges within universities—the college of science, the college of engineering, and so on—and each college has a number of faculty members who teach the courses (that is, a "faculty").

Ignore for now the differences between the two uses of "college," which are minor. This and other terms will become clear in a few more pages, as you begin to get a picture of American higher education.

INTERNATIONAL ENROLLMENT

Figure 1-2   International Students in Conversation *(Photo by Stephen Barnes)*

One reason your opportunities for study in the United States are so good is, simply, that there is a huge number of institutions of higher education in the country. Look briefly at the map in figure 1-3, which shows the state-by-state totals of such institutions, according to the most recent available survey. The state of New York alone has 326 of them; the state of California has 310. If you add all the figures together, the fifty states have some 3500 colleges and universities.

Figure 1-3   Numbers of Colleges and Universities by State, 1989–90

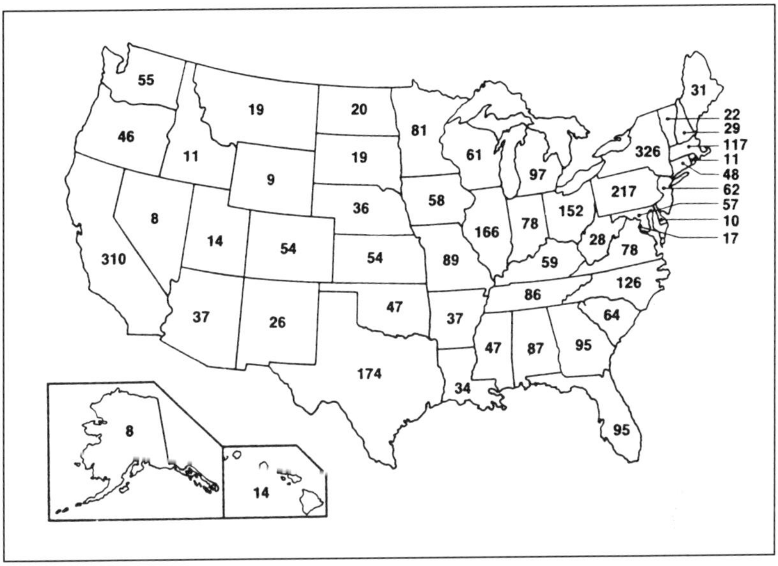

SOURCE: U.S. Dept. of Education, as reported in *The Chronicle of Higher Education Almanac,* September 5, 1990, p. 5.

And almost all these colleges and universities already have a substantial number of international students. Table 1-1 shows the 50 largest international enrollments in the country. At the top of the list is a community college (a two-year institution); most of the remaining institutions are universities, which is natural, because universities are usually much larger than colleges. Note that at the Massachusetts Institute of Technology—one of the leading technological institutions in the country—international students make up more than 20 percent of the total enrollment. Many other technical institutions, as well as small colleges, also have a high proportion of international students.

Table 1-1

Institutions with the Largest International Enrollments

Rank Institution	Number of foreign students	Proportion of total enrollment
1. Miami-Dade Community College	5,518	12.3%
2. University of Southern California	3,705	13.7%
3. University of Texas, Austin	3,588	7.1%
4. University of Wisconsin, Madison	3,295	7.5%
5. Boston University	3,248	11.4%
6. University of California, Los Angeles	3,126	8.6%
7. Ohio State University, main campus	2,887	5.5%
8. Columbia University	2,849	14.8%
9. University of Illinois, Urbana-Champaign	2,794	8.2%
10. University of Pennsylvania	2,778	13.7%
11. Southern Illinois University, Carbondale	2,615	10.6%
12. University of Minnesota, Minneapolis-St. Paul	2,555	4.4%
13. University of Michigan, Ann Arbor	2,465	6.8%
14. University of Maryland, College Park	2,397	6.7%
15. University of Houston, University Park	2,332	7.2%
16. Northeastern University	2,288	6.4%
17. Purdue University, main campus	2,277	6.4%
18. Michigan State University	2,270	5.3%
19. University of Arizona	2,253	6.4%
20. Harvard University	2,248	13.2%
21. George Washington University	2,207	11.6%
22. State University of New York, Buffalo	2,192	8.0%
23. Iowa State University	2,160	8.5%
24. Texas A&M University, main campus	2,156	5.3%
25. University of California, Berkeley	2,143	6.9%
26. Cornell University	2,138	11.3%
27. Arizona State University	2,005	6.8%
28. New York University	2,102	6.6%
29. Stanford University	2,081	15.6%
30. Indiana University, Bloomington	2,066	6.2%
31. Pennsylvania State University, main campus	2,059	5.5%
32. Massachusetts Institute of Technology	2,049	21.5%
33. California State University, Los Angeles	2,028	9.7%
34. Rutgers University	1,988	6.0%
35. University of Iowa	1,888	6.5%
36. University of Florida	1,880	5.5%
37. New Jersey Institute of Technology	1,864	23.9%
38. University of Hawaii, Manoa	1,850	10.2%
39. University of Kansas	1,837	7.0%
40. Oregon State University	1,817	11.4%

Table 1-1 (continued)

Rank Institution	Number of foreign students	Proportion of total enrollment
41. Brigham Young University	1,799	6.5%
42. University of Miami	1,756	12.6%
43. California State University, Long Beach	1,750	5.3%
44. University of Missouri	1,712	7.1%
45. University of Washington	1,661	5.1%
46. University of Toledo	1,640	6.9%
47. University of Massachusetts, Amherst	1,631	6.2%
48. Howard University	1,614	14.4%
49. Temple University	1,614	5.2%
50. San Francisco State University	1,611	5.5%

SOURCE: Institute for International Education, *Open Doors 1989/90*, pp. 66–67 (extrapolated from table 8.0).

Statistics indicate that, during the academic year 1989–90, there were nearly 390,000 international students in the United States, and that they were distributed among 2891 institutions. (Information about international enrollment comes from the Institute for International Education's annual publication *Open Doors*, which is listed in the Bibliography.) These totals do not include high schools or tertiary institutions with vocational curricula (schools for auto mechanics or computer programmers or secretaries or hairdressers). It is important to state that this book concentrates on college and university admission and does not address high school or vocational school admission directly, although the visa procedure is much the same for all students. You can be sure, however, that there are many international students in secondary and vocational schools too.

The total of 386,851 international students reported in *Open Doors 1989/90* can be broken into several categories: graduate students, 43.9%; undergraduates, 35.5%; students in associate-degree programs, 12.2%; and the remainder, in intensive English as a Second Language (ESL) programs or other categories. The most popular subject, among those enrolled at the college level, was business, closely followed by engineering.

Table 1-2 shows where most of these students came from. Asia accounted for more than half the international enrollment, and the number of Asians is increasing rapidly. But the totals for most of the other continents—for Europe, South America, and North America—are also increasing. Thus, higher education may be considered one of the United States' most important exports; American institutions enroll approximately one-third of the world's total international student population. Nearly 1 in 4 new Ph.D.'s awarded by American universities in the natural and computer sciences goes to an international student; in engineering fields, the ratio is 1 in 2.

Table 1-2
Leading Countries of Origin

Rank	Country or territory	Students
1.	China	33,390
2.	Taiwan	30,960
3.	Japan	29,840
4.	India	26,240
5.	Republic of Korea	21,710
6.	Canada	17,870
7.	Malaysia	14,110
8.	Hong Kong	11,230
9.	Indonesia	9,390
10.	Iran	7,440
11.	United Kingdom	7,100
12.	Pakistan	7,070
13.	West Germany	6,750
14.	Thailand	6,630
15.	Mexico	6,540
16.	France	5,340
17.	Jordan	5,250
18.	Philippines	4,540
19.	Nigeria	4,480
20.	Lebanon	4,450
21.	Singapore	4,440
22.	Greece	4,430
23.	Saudi Arabia	4,110
24.	Brazil	3,730
25.	Spain	3,640
26.	Turkey	3,400
27.	Colombia	3,320
28.	Israel	2,910
29.	Jamaica	2,850
30.	Peru	2,750

SOURCE: Institute for International Education, *Open Doors 1989/90*, p. 23.

INTERNATIONAL RECRUITMENT EFFORTS

Not surprisingly, most colleges and universities will admit you and other international students to study in their curricula, if you meet their academic and language standards and financial requirements. Many of these institutions are beginning to recruit students overseas. Increasingly, you will find American admissions officers touring your country, perhaps even visiting your schools, and leaving literature and videotapes promoting their institutions. The mails in your country are now full of catalogs and brochures and pamphlets and applications from American higher educational institutions.

Why is this so? Actually, there are several explanations. One is simply tradition. International students have been working on American campuses as long as most Americans can remember. A few universities and colleges were even founded as international institutions; these include the University of Miami (Florida) and Carthage International College (Illinois). But experts usually give two stronger reasons for the interest in international enrollments.

Internationalization

At one time, the United States was the most technologically advanced country in the world, and the richest. That situation has changed, of course. The exchange of technology among the industrial nations is important to all of them, and not least to the United States. In addition, there is a strong belief among college and university officials in the importance of diversity in the student population. The United States has many ethnic groups, some of which are not well represented on college and university campuses; additional enrollments from these groups, it is believed, will increase mutual understanding among them all. But international students also enrich the intellectual life of a campus—and *internationalization* is in fact a widely used word in higher education today.

Demographic Trends

The other reason given for the interest in international enrollments is that there are too few American students to fill the classrooms of more than 3000 colleges and universities. Most students leave secondary school at age 18, and at present, there are comparatively few 18-year-olds in the general population; thus, *more than 80 percent* of all colleges are currently unable to fill their freshman classes. Educators today also worry that American secondary school graduates are less well prepared than international students. Economic factors should be noted, as well: Today, many small institutions need to expand enrollments in order to survive; and a good way to expand and maintain quality is to recruit international students.

Besides these reasons, the colleges and universities are already well prepared to assist students from abroad. Because of the long history of the United States in international education, almost every college and university today has personnel who work professionally with international students. And it is scarcely more difficult to work with 200 international students, or 300, than to work with 100. The big universities, in fact, find it easy to provide services for 1500 international students when they already have 1000 and a long tradition of international education.

University Services to the International Community

What are these services that colleges and universities provide? This is the proper place to introduce you to the "international education establishment" in American higher education; the term refers to people whose professional duties are mostly, perhaps entirely, centered on people like you. For an example, we will consider a very large university—let us say, one with 30,000 students, of whom 1500 are from overseas—and review the professional personnel who work with these 1500.

First, there is the *foreign student advisor*. The title may vary from university to university; today, titles like *director of international services* or *director of international programs* are common. In this book, the traditional term will be used, or rather, the common abbreviation, FSA, and the office will be referred to as "International Services." At the university in our example, the FSA is (we will say) a woman who has studied overseas, traveled widely, and spent many years building expertise in international student affairs. She has a master's degree in a related field, such as international studies, educational administration, or counseling.

In the international services office, she has several people working for her, because a steady stream of international students comes into the office during the day. She also handles the problems of international faculty and staff members. We can assume that, at a university of 30,000 students, there are 400 teachers from overseas. Many of these people will have family members with them. The FSA's major responsibility is to see that all these persons from abroad—an international community of perhaps 2500 people—have their visas and other papers in order. She will also supervise international student associations, handle employment requests, work closely with the United States Immigration and Naturalization Service (INS), and keep the university informed of new INS policies. Whatever questions students may ask about their status, she will have heard them all before (and can probably answer most of them). She will be an extremely important person to her 2500 international faculty members and students throughout their stay in the United States.

Second, there is an *international admissions counselor;* in fact, this is the first person a new international student would come in contact with at this large university. We shall say that in our example this person is a man. If he has not lived overseas, he has probably traveled to many countries. He holds at least a bachelor's degree, and has acquired a good knowledge of education systems around the world. His major task, aside from recruiting, is to review the records of the students from other countries, looking for outstanding applicants, and to judge each student's ability to do work at his university. In short, his job is to bring people like you to his institution.

Several other people at the university teach English as a Second Language (ESL), perhaps in a special center or institution. ESL teachers have a variety of responsibilities within a university. Usually, their most common activity is in the intensive program—the set of courses for students who are studying only English, as they attempt to meet this university's (or another institution's) entrance requirements. ESL teachers will also probably provide teacher training to international teaching assistants (overseas graduate students who support themselves by teaching undergraduate classes for the university). They may be the instructors of special ESL sections of required undergraduate courses—for example, freshman composition. In some universities, they run special programs for outside groups, such as a business English course for foreign-born people working in industry.

There are other experts on international student matters at the university, whether or not they work full-time at such matters. The personnel office will have at least one official who knows the immigration laws that deal with international students' employment. Someone in the housing office will know what sort of living accommodations are appropriate to, or popular with, students from other countries. Academic departments or colleges may assign persons to take care of international student concerns. Doctors at the student health clinic will be reasonably sophisticated about the medical problems newcomers bring from overseas.

In addition, the community around the university may have a volunteer organization whose purpose is to help make your stay in that community pleasant. These groups arrange trips, home stays, holiday get-togethers, international fashion shows, and other orientation events; they may also promote talks by international visitors to students in the local schools. Or these activities may be organized by a local ''International House,'' a residence for overseas students whose goal is to promote international understanding.

All these organizations and individuals are still only part of the international education establishment. Many other people at the university, for example, work to help Americans study abroad or to set up American-style colleges overseas; more than 60,000 American students attend universities in other countries. A large university will have a foreign languages department with international faculty, and perhaps sister institution relationships with universities abroad. A new emphasis on multiculturalism means that a university will probably have courses on African, Asian, and Native American cultures taught by faculty from other parts of the United States and from other countries.

International teaching assistants and research assistants may be added to the list, for they carry out a large part of the university's academic work. But we will discuss their positions later. It should be clear enough, already, that the American university is a large international organization. Most of the smaller colleges are also in the process of internationalizing their campuses. The general attitude of American higher education has been stated as follows, by the College Entrance Examination Board:

> Institutions of higher education in the United States welcome foreign students. Their presence helps to promote international understanding, and in the long run, makes for a more orderly and peaceful world. In addition, American education is enriched by the academic and cultural contribution of foreign students.
> —*Entering Higher Education in the United States*, p. 7

Preparing to Meet Your Goals

Obviously, you have an opportunity. If you want to study in the United States, and you have demonstrated academic ability, the chances are good that you can find a way to achieve your goal. The first question to ask yourself is whether a degree from the United States will truly aid your career. Some countries give little recognition to American degrees. In such a situation, you would be wise to do your university work at home or in a third country.

But if you have decided, for good reasons, to pursue studies in the United States, your preparation can begin. The first step is to gain a basic understanding of American education, primary and secondary as well as tertiary, and the way a college or university functions. These matters are considered in chapter 2. In later chapters, we will address questions like these: How can you choose an appropriate college or university? What admission requirements must be met? How can you make the application process work for you? Are there ways to finance your studies? How can you avoid problems in getting your visa? What arrangements can you make in advance of your arrival, so that moving to the United States will go smoothly? Then, the last few chapters discuss life *after* your move—after your arrival at an American campus. The final goal of this book is to make your adjustment to your new situation as pleasant as possible.

Now the responsibility is yours, in two ways. You need to follow the steps that the book lays out, and that means doing considerable research. Many hours of work lie ahead. It may take you several months simply to identify the institutions to which you want to apply.

It is also your responsibility to work hard at your current studies. If you are still attending classes, you must try to achieve high marks. If you are no longer a student, you must show that you have academic potential. And in either case, you must develop your mastery of English. No college or university wants you to come several thousand miles only to fail because you lack the necessary academic skills.

Work to the level of your potential, choose the right kind of institutions, and good fortune may follow. In all likelihood, there is a college, a university, or other institution in the United States that will be a good place for you to study.

PART I

GETTING READY

CHAPTER 2

UNDERSTANDING AMERICAN EDUCATION

WHAT DO COLLEGES AND UNIVERSITIES IN THE UNITED STATES LOOK like? How do they work? What educational backgrounds do the students have when they arrive on campus? We will draw together the important answers to those questions here, although they are certainly not simple questions. You have read that the international student enrollment is spread over nearly 3000 institutions. The variety to be found in these institutions is enormous, but there are several common factors that can be reported.

The place to start is with the students themselves and their educational background. We will take a quick look at American primary and secondary education and follow that with a summary of American educational philosophy, before we turn our attention once again to colleges and universities. You will see patterns in the lower schools that will appear again in undergraduate and graduate education.

"K–12"

Diversity is natural in American education, because of the country's size, its extremes of huge cities and remote wilderness areas, and its long history of mass education. All these factors make general truths about education difficult to state. And yet there is remarkable uniformity in certain features of the educational system. Even the terminology is generally the same across the country.

Preschool, for example, refers to the organized activities of children four years of age and younger. "Kindergarten" (the "K" in "K–12") is the preparation for schooling that children undertake at age 5. Then they all enter "grade school" (sometimes called "primary" or "grammar" school), in the first grade.

The divisions and standards of school systems throughout the nation also follow a similar pattern. Typically, children will leave grade school after six years, at age 12, and enter "junior high school" (although there are alternative "middle school" programs). After three years in junior high they move on to "senior high school" for their final three years. They will graduate at the age of 17 or 18, at which point they (or rather, the academically gifted among them) are ready to enter a college or university. In sum, their schooling always lasts twelve years.

The vast majority of the primary and secondary schools in all the states are public, although there is a sizable number of private schools. The public schools are administered by local governmental agencies. The United States federal government has very little role in the administration of K–12 schools. State governments do set standards and provide about 50 percent of the funding, but day-to-day control is in the hands of a "school board," which represents the local community. Private schools may be operated by religious groups or as private organizations, but their curricula are very similar to those in the public schools.

Schooling in the United States is usually mandatory to the age of 16. Currently, some 48 million students are enrolled in primary and secondary schools. The literacy rate is high; approximately 75 percent of all students receive their high school diplomas, and nearly 60 percent of those who graduate from high school enter college— that is, tertiary education.

AMERICAN EDUCATIONAL PHILOSOPHY

American educational philosophy is reflected in the structure of the primary/secondary system and in the content of the curricula. First, there is a strong belief in the United States that religion and government should be separated. Thus, the majority of students attend public schools, where religious instruction, or organized prayer, is not permitted. The public school system also reflects American democratic ideals, for it educates all children together: girls and boys; the very bright and the slow learners; Catholics, Protestants, Jews, and members of other religious groups; whites, African-Americans, Hispanics, and Asian-Americans.

Second, Americans believe that their high schools should be comprehensive—that is, that their curricula should cover all subjects appropriate to secondary education. Thus, classical subjects like languages, literature, and mathematics are offered alongside manual arts, physical education, typing, bookkeeping, and other practical courses. An emphasis on practicality is, in fact, the most obvious feature of American educational philosophy. Children are expected to be able to *do* things, not simply to know about them. They are also encouraged to be "well-rounded" or "whole persons"—young people who have social and physical skills, as well as intellectual skills.

Figure 2-1   Mary Reed Building, University of Denver *(Photo provided courtesy of University of Denver)*

One result of this emphasis on the complete person is that children usually graduate from high school having a little knowledge about a great many things but not much knowledge about any one subject. You will see this lack of specialized knowledge among undergraduates, and especially among freshmen. American educators have often expressed concern over the emphasis on breadth rather than depth. Very few high school graduates, for example, have learned a foreign language well. Most have not taken mathematics beyond algebra. Their competence in the sciences is low, particularly when measured against high school graduates from many other countries. And so on.

On the other hand, American high school graduates have usually learned how to learn—how to begin teaching themselves new subjects. It is true that they have fallen behind their peers in other countries, during their K–12 years. But they have time to catch up, because so many college opportunities are available to them. Indeed, nearly 25 percent of young adults in the United States now complete four years of post-secondary education.

COLLEGE/UNIVERSITY MODELS IN THE UNITED STATES

Naturally, similarities in philosophy can be found between the K–12 system and the college/university system. Thus, the pace of specialization is slow at colleges and universities too; the curricula range far beyond the classical subjects to new technical fields like radio broadcasting, computer systems operations, and hospitality industry management; the practical is as important as the theoretical in the sciences, where laboratory requirements are extensive. People are also admitted to institutions of higher learning irrespective of their age, sex, race, religion, or national background.

These are common features of higher education. But distinctions between institutions can be made. To begin, they may be divided into five types:

- *Doctoral-level institutions*. In this category you will find most of the universities whose names you already know. These are the large research universities. The majority of them are public institutions, and many of them were founded by the individual states—e.g., the University of Arizona, the University of Missouri, the University of Delaware—to serve the people of those states. But several of the most distinguished are private: Chicago, Harvard, Princeton, Stanford, and Yale, to name only a few.

- *Comprehensive institutions.* These universities resemble those in the first category except that they usually offer no degree higher than the master's; it follows that, generally, they are not so large.

- *General baccalaureate institutions.* As the title implies, this category contains the small colleges—institutions that offer courses in a general field of study (usually liberal arts) and award no degrees higher than a bachelor's degree.

- *Specialized institutions.* This term designates a category of business or professional schools, sometimes post-graduate; examples include medical and law schools and theological seminaries.

- *Two-year institutions.* This is the largest category (nearly 1500 colleges), for it contains all the community colleges that have been organized across the country in the last thirty years; we will look more closely at community colleges in a moment. Two-year colleges offer the associate's degree. Graduates are usually (but not always) able to transfer their work into four-year schools.

Of the total number of colleges and universities (about 3300), some 1800 are privately supported.

A few words must be said about the community colleges and their role in international education. As the name indicates, these institutions were founded by, and for, communities across the country. Their curricula reflect, in part, local labor needs. Thus, in a coastal city, the community college might have a fisheries program; in an automotive center, the curricula might include welding and industrial design; and so on. Tuition charges are kept low, in order to encourage local high school graduates to continue their education. For all these reasons, community colleges tend not to recruit international students or even students from other cities and counties.

Yet one can say that there are international students in all categories of institutions, including community colleges. Before you apply to one, you should simply be sure that international applications will be accepted. You will also want to compare advantages and disadvantages of studying at a community college with those of studying at other institutions. These will be reviewed in chapter 3.

THE CAMPUS

By tradition, colleges and universities are located in pastoral, or rural, settings. Some state universities were intentionally founded in towns or small cities, rather than in urban centers; many other institutions were built *near,* but not *in,* urban areas. And those institutions located within cities are often set apart by large, park-like grounds. The University of Chicago, shown in the figure 2-2, provides an example, for it is situated near downtown Chicago, whose metropolitan area contains 8 million people.

Figure 2-2 Looking Northeast from the University of Chicago Campus to Downtown Chicago *(Jim Wright/The University of Chicago)*

University architecture also has a distinctive style. The combination of academic buildings and park-like grounds usually sets a college or university apart from its surroundings, and is known as the campus. Thus the term *on-campus* is used to designate whatever occurs (or stands) on the university's own property. The extent of the campus can be enormous, and may include a farm, various gar-

Figure 2-3 Map of University of Wisconsin Campus (Madison)

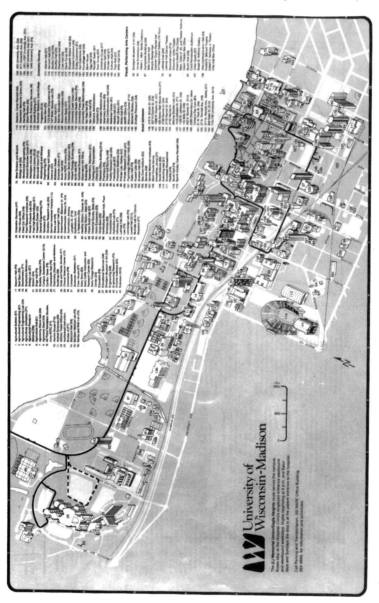

SOURCE: Courtesy of News and Information Service, University of Wisconsin–Madison

dens, a stadium and other sports buildings, ''skyscraper'' dormitories, a pond or a river, and even a shopping mall; traveling the various roads on the campus, you may see stoplights—needed to control traffic—and the university's own buses, used to move large groups of students. Figure 2-3 shows a map of the University of Wisconsin–Madison campus and gives some idea of the scale and diversity of such institutions.

An American university is in fact a city in itself. It fulfills most human needs: Students can eat there, sleep there, plant flowers or buy flowers there, get treated for an illness, go bowling, see a travel agent, play a variety of sports, or get a haircut—right on the campus. All this activity and diversity may surprise you. The American concept of the ''whole person'' suggests, however, that there would naturally be a great many student services and student activities at any college or university.

ADMINISTRATIVE STRUCTURE

Now that you have a ''picture'' of the campus, it is time to talk about the way the university works. Obviously, it is not just an academic enterprise—not just a few classrooms and teachers. Someone, for example, has to provide direction for all those student activities discussed above. A university (and to a lesser degree, a college) is in fact a complex organization. You need to know the academic activities best, but you should also have an understanding of the total structure. Begin by reviewing figure 2-4 on page 25.

Universities have considerable independence; there is no ''ministry of education,'' and little direct governmental control, even in governmentally supported institutions. The final responsibility for directing the operations of an American university lies in the hands of a *board of trustees* (or *board of regents*). This is a committee of citizens who meet only occasionally to approve new policies for the university, and you will probably never see them. The chief administrative officer is the president (sometimes the ''chancellor''), whom you may see, but only occasionally and at formal events. Usually, this person spends much of his or her time off campus, promoting the university's name and raising money, which is a strict necessity today for all university presidents. Day-to-day operations may be supervised by the vice-presidents, especially by the provost, who is a sort of senior vice-president.

As in a large corporation, the vice-presidents direct the major administrative functions of the university. Five such functions can be identified as fundamental to any university's successful operation:

- *Instructional activities,* which will be supervised by the provost or vice-president for academic affairs
- The *student services operation,* which will be under the direction of a vice-president for student life/services/activities
- *Financial operations,* which include collecting university revenues, supervising moneymaking activities such as the bookstore, and balancing the budget, and which will be the responsibility of the treasurer (or an equivalent vice-president)
- *Fund-raising*—the constant effort to bring in money from alumni, large corporations, charitable foundations, and wealthy individuals—which is overseen by a vice-president for development
- *Maintenance* of the university's physical plant, which is supervised by a vice-president for "facilities management," or a person with a similar title

Each of these vice-presidents supervises several directors and other personnel. It takes many people to manage a "small city," and the administrative staff of an American university often outnumbers the faculty.

ACADEMIC STRUCTURE

Under the provost or vice-president for academic affairs we find quite a few people whose work is also mainly administrative. For instance, the next level down in the academic line consists of the deans, who supervise the colleges. A college within a university is similar to the other type of college we have discussed. Part of the definition given in chapter 1 was that a college offers baccalaureate

Figure 2-4 The American University: A Typical Organizational
Structure

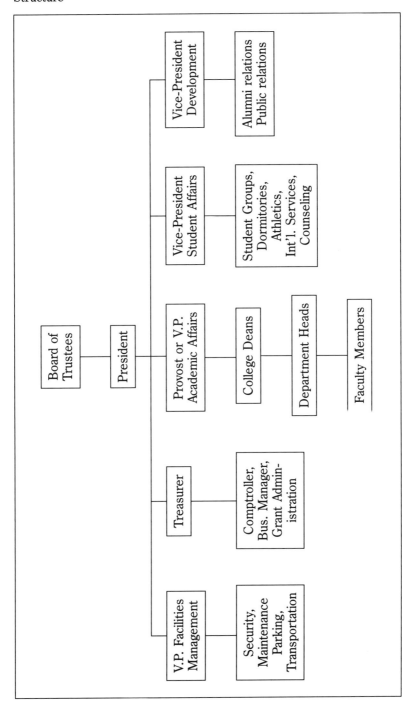

degrees "in one large area of study such as the liberal arts." That part is also true of colleges within a university, which supervise broad areas of study such as business administration, engineering, arts and sciences, and the like. The difference is that, in a university, these colleges will also offer master's and other advanced degrees.

The colleges are then divided into departments. A college of business administration, for example, usually has departments of accounting, economics, finance, marketing, and statistics, among others; a college of engineering may be organized into the structure shown in figure 2-5. Each department has its own faculty (teachers) and its own department head, who may be elected by the faculty or appointed by the dean. The department head has full academic qualifications and will probably teach one or two courses a term. Deans almost always have Ph.D.'s as well, and will teach at least occasionally.

In a typical university, the faculty are divided into three ranks: Professor, Associate Professor, and Assistant Professor. The first two titles carry tenure, or assurance of continued employment; the purpose of tenure is to allow faculty to conduct research in areas of their own choosing, and to report the results of their research, no matter how controversial or unpopular their findings may be. Assistant professors are usually on "tenure track," meaning that they are completing a probationary period—typically, seven years. Tenure is most often awarded on the basis of significant research and publication, although good teaching performance, the ability to raise grant money, and service (to either the department, the university, or the community) will also be considered.

If you enter an American university as a freshman (first-year) or sophomore (second-year) student, however, you may find very few of these professors teaching you. Thus, two other categories of instructional staff—the ones freshmen most often see—deserve mention. First, many universities employ part-time teachers, who are not voting members of the faculty. These teachers are collectively called the "adjunct faculty," and individually called "instructors" or "lecturers" (although the latter term is comparatively rare in the United States).

Many other instructors in introductory courses are teaching assistants (TAs). These are actually students themselves—graduate students who support their studies by teaching lower-level courses

Figure 2-5   Typical College Organization
(Example: College of Engineering)

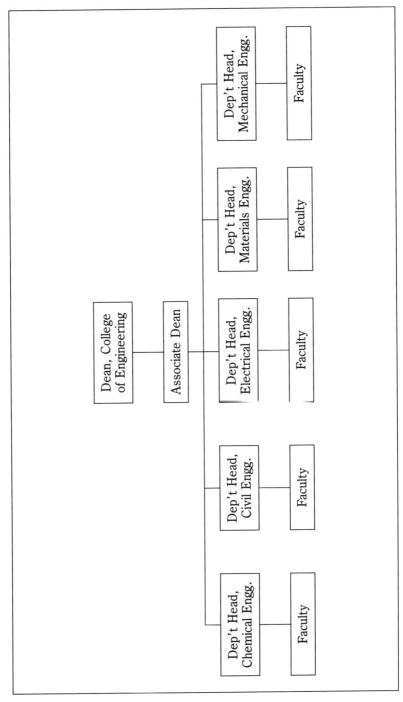

in their departments. This "apprentice" system is very well established and very widespread, although it is not always popular with undergraduate students. Because many TAs come from overseas, we will speak more about them when we review the problem of financing your education, in chapter 6.

Small, independent colleges do not, of course, have all these personnel. In the academic line, there may be a single dean, who reports directly to the president. There are no teaching assistants, because there are no graduate students. There may be an adjunct faculty, but the full-time faculty carry most of the teaching load. Colleges are in fact sometimes distinguished from universities as "teaching institutions" rather than "research institutions."

REQUIREMENTS

As you read through the following chapters, you will discover, little by little, the "Americanness" of certain features of higher education in the United States—including several that Americans themselves probably do not recognize as peculiar to their own culture. Some of these features will require understanding and acceptance on your part. In closing this introduction to American higher education, we need to discuss two of these: distribution requirements and the credit system. They are among the most important for you to understand if you have decided to apply to an American college or university, particularly at the undergraduate level.

Distribution Requirements

You have read that specialization comes slowly in American education. International freshmen are often surprised, in fact, that they will take few courses in their major fields during the first year of study. Instead, they must take "general education" courses, also referred to as *distribution requirements*. Typically, all freshmen must enroll in a series of courses in English (writing and literature), mathematics, and the sciences; probably they will be expected to take one or more history or social science classes and physical education classes as well. Thus, freshmen enrollments are "distributed" among various departments.

Distribution requirements reflect that concern for the whole person mentioned early in this chapter. For the same reason, some colleges and universities require their students to complete a "minor" as well as a "major." The major is the concentration, or specialization, in a single subject area; the minor consists of a few courses in a (perhaps) totally different subject. Students choose their major and minor fields, of course, and usually have some choice of subjects. The distribution requirement, on the other hand, generally causes them to take courses well removed from their immediate interests.

The Credit System

> The elective system reflects the freedom to choose any direction and orientation. The student feels more involved in the life of the university and it is an opportunity for him/her to get a general culture.
>
> —A student from France

The second important feature is the system of academic credits for coursework. Let us say that you have decided to transfer from a university in your country to an American institution. At least some of the courses taken at your first university will be accepted as counting toward an American baccalaureate degree. Their worth will be measured in credits—in your case, in "transfer credits." Almost every college and university in the United States uses the credit system, and it is important to understand how it works.

A credit is usually awarded for every hour of lecture a student attends in a course each week; a history course meeting one hour on each of three days (for example, Mondays, Wednesdays, and Fridays) is, logically, a 3-credit course. Laboratory work, by contrast, is measured as one credit for every two hours of instruction. Thus, a chemistry course that has three hours of lecture each week and two hours of lab work counts as a 4-credit course. (Note: There is also the question of *semester* versus *quarter* credits, which will be discussed in chapter 5.)

What is the purpose of credits? To determine the answer, we may look once more at distribution requirements for an example. Freshmen, we have said, must take science courses even when they are not science majors. But perhaps they have a choice of sciences: They might be able to choose among biology, chemistry, and physics. Of, if they must take 6 credits in chemistry, they might have a choice of chemistry courses by which to reach the total of 6. Similarly, all students may be required to take, say, 15 credits of electives, but they can choose any courses they want to build the total to 15. The credit system is a way of counting the student's steps toward graduation. Typically, those steps add up to 128 credits completed over eight semesters. See table 2-1 for a sample distribution of credits toward graduation.

Table 2-1
Sample Distribution of Graduation Credits
(Total Credits = 128)

Year	Semester	Distribution	Major	Minor	Electives
Freshman	1	16			
Freshman	2	13	3		
Sophomore	1	3	9		3
Sophomore	2	3	8	3	3
Junior	1		9	3	6
Junior	2		6	9	2
Senior	1		6	6	3
Senior	2		8	2	4

Thus far we have looked only at the undergraduate system. But credits also measure the progress of graduate students. A master's degree typically requires 30 to 36 semester credits, and doctoral requirements usually include another 30 to 36 credits. The idea that a student must complete a certain number of units in a given subject is, in fact, firmly embedded in all layers of education in the United States.

SUMMARY

> In getting your scope achieved, to find the right American college or university, I believe that you have to know yourself, to know better what ... you want, to be sure about and clear about your desire....
>
> —A student from Romania

There are many more features of American higher education for you to understand, but you will master them as you continue your research. You now have an outline of an institution of higher education in the United States. It has a campus; it has a number of services and activities besides instruction; it has curricula in which specialization at undergraduate level arrives slowly; and it has a credit system that determines students' progress toward their degrees. If you are confident that pursuing an education in the United States should be your goal—if you are ''sure about and clear about your desire''—it is now time to begin considering which of the thousands of colleges and universities you should apply to.

CHAPTER 3

CHOOSING THE RIGHT SCHOOL

"WHERE ARE YOU GOING TO COLLEGE?" YOUNG PEOPLE IN THE UNITED States often ask each other. "Are you in school somewhere?" In these American expressions, "college" simply means higher education, rather than a small institution offering only a baccalaureate degree; it can even refer to graduate study. And "school," a term that in most countries refers to primary or secondary education, can mean a community college, a liberal arts college, a university, an English language program, a professional school, a vocational training program, or an institute of technology.

This chapter is intended to help you answer the question "Where are you going to 'college'?" Obviously, you have a great variety of "schools" to choose from, whether your objective is a graduate school, undergraduate study, or an ESL program. We will look at each of these objectives later, but first, two more general topics must be considered: (1) where to find information on American institutions of learning, and (2) which criteria you need to consider in selecting the right institution.

SOURCES OF INFORMATION

Choosing the best educational program is difficult even for those who live in the United States. Unless you have been to the United States, or have friends who know the country's educational system, you may wonder where to start your research. But help is probably available close to home. In many countries today, English language bookstores—or special sections of other bookstores—carry guides to American higher education. Your government's education department or ministry may also be able to offer advice.

Your school or university can probably provide help as well. If you are still in secondary school, you may get good advice from an educational counselor. If you have studied at a university, there are even more sources of help available, for the university library may have many reference works on American educational institutions. Your professors are likely to understand the American system well. If you are hoping to become a graduate student in the United States, then your major professors will be, indeed, your *best* source of advice.

AMERICAN AGENCIES

> How does a student in my country ... find the right
> American university? The best way is [that] a student go
> to the USIS office. I don't exactly know what USIS
> stands for. As I know, it is the office for a student who
> wants to study in America.
> —A student from Indonesia

Eventually, you will want to visit official American agencies in your country. Your first thought might be to go to the American embassy, or perhaps an American consulate. But these are not usually the places to start. The embassy is where all the contacts between your government and the American government are managed. Within an embassy, the Consular Division handles visas; a consulate is a separate office in a provincial city whose principal function is to issue visas. In large countries whose relations with the United States are intensive and extensive, these agencies are usually too busy to provide college counseling.

Most often, the best starting place is the United States Information Service (USIS), a government agency located in almost every city in the world where there is a consulate. Although USIS offices may not always offer a college advisory service, they have libraries that contain a wealth of general information about the United States. USIS also publishes many materials of use to prospective

international students. In particular, you should ask for a free series of brochures titled *If You Want to Study in the United States*,
and other materials.

The USIS library will probably stock various college guides published annually; figure 3-1 contains a representative list of these
publications. You may not be ready, at this point, to study them.
While certainly useful as summaries, and for purposes of comparison, the guides necessarily contain an enormous amount of infor-

Figure 3-1   A Guide to College Guides, with Ordering Information

Admissions Requirements for International Students (1986)
   Two Trees Press, P.O. Box 819040, Fargo, ND 58102 USA

The College Handbook
The College Handbook: Foreign Student Supplement
The College Handbook for Transfer Students
   College Entrance Examination Board, 45 Columbus
   Avenue, New York, NY 10023 USA

Comparative Guide to American Colleges for Students,
Parents, and Counselors
   Harper & Row, 10 E. 53rd St., New York, NY 10022
   USA

Directory of Graduate Programs
   Graduate Record Examinations Board, c/o Educational
   Testing Service, CN 6000, Princeton, NJ 08541 USA

English Language and Orientation Programs in the United
States
   IIE Books, Institute of International Education, 809
   United Nations Plaza, New York, NY 10017-3580 USA

Graduate and Professional Programs: An Overview
Guide to Four-Year Colleges
Guide to Two-Year Colleges
   Peterson's Guides, Inc., P.O. Box 2123, Princeton, NJ
   08543-2123 USA

The Insider's Guide to the Colleges
   St. Martin's Press, 175 Fifth Avenue, New York, NY
   10010 USA

Lovejoy's College Guide
   Lovejoy's Educational Guides, P.O. Box Q, Red Bank, NJ
   07701 USA

Profiles of American Colleges
   Barron's Educational Series, P.O. Box 8040, 250 Wireless
   Blvd., Hauppauge, NY 11788 USA

mation. All the data are condensed—sometimes, reduced to abbreviations—and they can be confusing. Thus, you may want to come back to the guides after you have gone further in your research. When you do look at them, you might well begin with *The College Handbook: Foreign Student Supplement,* which provides a comparatively easy reference to costs and admission requirements at more than 2000 institutions.

EDUCATIONAL ADVISING CENTERS

In the world's large capital cities, college advising is usually carried out by a designated "educational advising center"—perhaps an office of the Institute for International Education or the Fulbright Commission or another binational organization. In Appendix 1, you will find the locations of approximately 275 educational advising centers located in more than 140 countries around the world. USIS prepares a "Minimum Reference Bookshelf" for each center's use; it includes several of the books shown in figure 3-1 or mentioned in this chapter. The current titles are reproduced in Appendix 2, so that you may see how much information is available to students who are prepared to do their research. The Minimum Reference Bookshelf is regularly updated. By looking through books and brochures mentioned in it, you will find answers to many of your questions.

The educational advising centers offer a wide range of services, facilities, and information as well as a library. They may include the following:

- A reading room where guests can review a complete collection of college and university catalogs—graduate and undergraduate—and ESL program brochures
- A student advisory service newsletter in the language of your country
- Guest lectures at local secondary schools
- Sample form letters that can be used at various stages in the application process
- Posted lists of tuition charges at colleges and universities

- A recorded message for telephone callers who want to know about the visa procedure
- Handouts with detailed descriptions of popular curricula (e.g., computer science) available in the United States, and lists of institutions that offer them
- Videotapes of the visa procedure, narrated in the language of the country
- Presentations by returning students
- Small-group discussion sessions
- Predeparture orientation sessions on American culture
- Computer programs that enable you to sort through a large number of institutions until you narrow the list to those that meet your needs

Small offices probably cannot provide many of these services. There, however, you may be able to speak personally with an expert. (Note: Budget problems have forced some USIS offices to limit their advising services. Even in very large cities, a USIS office may have a single educational advisor who works only a few hours per week and only nine or ten months a year. You should not expect to walk into a USIS office and get immediate advice.)

One last point: Watch for ''college fairs''—huge recruiting sessions where representatives of numerous educational institutions (sometimes Canadian, Australian, and British as well as American) come together to distribute their literature. These may be arranged by the USIS, the educational advising center, a local organization, or even a local educational recruiting agent; perhaps they will occur only in your country's capital city and only once a year, but they are very worthwhile. In two or three hours, you can learn as much about American colleges and universities as you can in a month of reading catalogs and directories.

GENERAL CRITERIA TO CONSIDER

The most important factor in your choice of an institution—whether graduate, undergraduate, or ESL—is of course the academic one. You need to find a program that matches your academic needs, abilities, and wishes. But a number of other criteria are worth your consideration. At least they may help you narrow the field of choices, and we will review them here.

Institutional Size

Institutions of higher learning in the United States vary in enrollment size from tiny to enormous, and you should consider just how large a student body will be right for you. Of course, applicants for graduate study understand that they will end up in a fairly big place—a research university—while applicants to ESL programs are sure to end up in a fairly small operation. Still, there are differences between tiny and small enrollments, and between large and huge enrollments. And applicants for undergraduate study, in particular, have a very wide range of enrollment sizes to choose from.

It should already be clear that some universities are very big indeed. Table 3-1 lists the names and enrollments of the forty-five largest, according to the latest available statistics. These are truly "cities," as we described campuses in chapter 2. By contrast, most ESL programs and many colleges enroll fewer than 1000 students; a number of highly regarded colleges have fewer than 2000 students.

Good arguments can be made for both small and large schools. In a small school, the emphasis is usually on teaching; even in freshman and sophomore courses, your teachers will be the full-time professors. The classes may be smaller and individual attention, both from the teaching and administrative staff, is more likely. The overall atmosphere is perhaps friendlier.

On the other hand, the large university will have more services for you as well as more people from your own part of the world. The international establishment is better equipped to meet your needs. The choice of majors will be larger, and so will the choice of courses within the major. And a degree from a large institution has a better chance of being recognized back in your home country.

Think carefully, then, about the question of small versus big. Probably, the size of your previous educational institutions will suggest where you might be most comfortable.

Table 3-1
The 45 Largest Colleges and Universities, by Enrollment (1988)

School	Enrollment
University of Minnesota–Twin Cities	61,556
Ohio State University main campus	53,661
University of Texas at Austin	50,106
Michigan State University	44,480
Miami-Dade Community College	43,880
Arizona State University	43,426
University of Wisconsin at Madison	43,364
Texas A&M University	39,163
University of Illinois at Urbana-Champaign	38,337
Pennsylvania State University main campus	37,269
University of Maryland at College Park	36,681
Purdue University main campus	36,517
University of Michigan at Ann Arbor	36,001
University of Arizona	34,725
University of California at Los Angeles	34,371
San Diego State University	34,155
Indiana University at Bloomington	33,776
University of Washington	33,460
University of Florida	33,282
California State University at Long Beach	33,179
Rutgers University at New Brunswick	32,901
Northeastern University	32,385
Temple University	32,139
Northern Virginia Community College	31,896
Macomb Community College	31,462
University of Cincinnati main campus	31,432
University of Southern California	30,831
Wayne State University	30,751
New York University	30,750
University of Houston–University Park	30,372
St. Louis Community College	30,291
Houston Community College	30,236
Brigham Young University main campus	30,226
University of California at Berkeley	30,102
University of Iowa	30,001
University of South Florida	29,912
California State University at Northridge	29,401
Boston University	28,555
University of Pittsburgh main campus	28,524
State University of New York at Buffalo	28,005
University of Massachusetts at Amherst	27,918
University of Akron main campus	27,818
Louisiana State University	27,348
University of Georgia	27,176
Oakland Community College	26,854

SOURCE: U.S. Department of Education, *Chronicle of Higher Education Almanac,* September 5, 1990, p. 20.

Population Density

You may also have a preference about the population of the town or city in which you study. By comparison with other peoples, Americans have been used to having a lot of space. An overseas visitor is usually struck by the "elbow room," or personal space, that is enjoyed by residents of the United States, and the amount of privacy this space makes possible for them. Nevertheless there are heavily crowded areas of the country as well as wide open spaces, and you will have no trouble finding the proper environment, whether town or city.

Table 3-2 lists the fifty largest cities in the United States, by order of estimated population; note that the stated population would often be twice as large if the "metropolitan area" residents were counted. You may be sure that each metropolitan area has several colleges (even small colleges) and universities. On the other hand,

Table 3-2
The 50 Largest Cities in the United States, by Population

City	Population	City	Population
New York, NY	7,262,700	Nashville–Davidson, TN	473,670
Los Angeles, CA	3,259,340	Austin, TX	466,550
Chicago, IL	3,009,530	Oklahoma City, OK	446,120
Houston, TX	1,728,910	Kansas City, MO	441,170
Philadelphia, PA	1,642,900	Fort Worth, TX	429,550
Detroit, MI	1,086,220	St. Louis, MO	426,300
San Diego, CA	1,015,190	Atlanta, GA	421,910
Dallas, TX	1,003,520	Long Beach, CA	396,280
San Antonio, TX	914,350	Portland, OR	387,870
Phoenix, AZ	894,070	Pittsburgh, PA	387,490
Baltimore, MD	752,800	Miami, FL	373,940
San Francisco, CA	749,000	Tulsa, OK	373,750
Indianapolis, IN	719,820	Honolulu, HI	372,330
San Jose, CA	712,080	Cincinnati, OH	369,750
Memphis, TN	652,640	Albuquerque, NM	366,750
Washington, DC	626,000	Tucson, AZ	358,850
Jacksonville, FL	609,860	Oakland, CA	356,960
Milwaukee, WI	605,090	Minneapolis, MN	356,840
Boston, MA	573,600	Charlotte, NC	352,070
Columbus, OH	566,030	Omaha, NE	349,270
New Orleans, LA	554,500	Toledo, OH	340,680
Cleveland, OH	535,830	Virginia Beach, VA	333,400
Denver, CO	505,000	Buffalo, NY	324,820
El Paso, TX	491,800	Sacramento, CA	323,550
Seattle, WA	486,200	Newark, NJ	316,240

SOURCE: *Information Please Almanac, Atlas & Yearbook* (Boston: Houghton Mifflin, 1990), p. 787.

large universities may be located in comparatively small cities. The famous "Big 10" universities of the Midwest provide several examples: The universities of Illinois, Indiana, and Iowa all have enrollments of between 30,000 and 40,000 students, but are located in cities with fewer than 200,000 residents.

A large university provides many cultural benefits for a small city (and for its students). But it is fair to say that the major cities of the United States will best satisfy you if you want to be near excellent cultural institutions, transportation facilities, industry, and commerce. They have another advantage, in that you will almost certainly find a community of people from your own country there.

Certain large American cities, it is true, have the reputation of being "dangerous," and with some reason; international students who live there have to make adjustments. But it must be added that suburbs, towns, and rural areas have their own problems. They are also less internationally minded. You might be the only person in town who speaks your language and find few people who have a good understanding of the outside world. It is possible that you would have more *physical* security in a small town, but more *emotional* security in a city.

Actually, you are likely to be happy wherever you go—whether city, town, or village. They all have their good features. But the question of urban versus small-town life is an important one. So are

Figure 3-2   The Philadelphia Skyline

broader cultural questions—for the various regions of the United States do have their own cultures. You should plan on reading about the social history of the region you are considering; if possible, talk to people in your country who have lived there.

Educational and Living Expenses

For most students, the tuition and other costs of a university or college are an important factor in their decision to seek admission. Many of them are surprised that higher education in the United States is so expensive. They may be used to a system where education is free—but then, only the very brightest people are admitted. In the United States, the system is based on the country's traditions of democracy and free enterprise. Many people can find admission to higher education, but they are expected to pay a large portion of the cost.

But it is incorrect to think that all institutions of higher learning have extremely high tuition. To be sure, the most expensive schools now charge undergraduates more than US$10,000 in tuition each academic year, but other colleges and universities are quite affordable. Community colleges may charge only a few hundred dollars' tuition per term, and even the large public universities have reasonable rates. Each September, the College Entrance Examination Board publishes a guide to tuition at 2500 institutions; you will find the current edition under "Sources."

The tuition for graduate education is higher than that for undergraduate or ESL study, and properly so: The investment that a university makes in its graduate programs—from distinguished faculty to advanced research facilities—is much greater. On the other hand, the chances of finding financial assistance are substantially better for graduate students (and we will discuss these opportunities in chapter 6). A graduate degree is also an excellent investment on the student's part, because usually, it vastly increases his or her earning potential.

One other factor to consider is the so-called "cost of living." As in most countries, cities in the United States tend to be more expensive to live in than small towns. Generally, the cost of living is also higher in the northern part of the country than in the southern part, and the East tends to be more expensive than the West, with the major exception of California. But these generalizations are too large and you should make inquiries of your own. In addition, because your education in the United States is an investment in your future, finding the "cheapest place" should not be your goal.

Housing Accommodations

Although housing will not be your main consideration, it is still an important criterion in determining your final choice of a college or university. First, which institutions offer on-campus housing? Two-year colleges—particularly community colleges—often do not, whereas four-year colleges usually do and universities almost certainly do. Be sure to find the answer about the institutions that interest you; you want the *option* of living in a college or university dormitory, even if you currently prefer the idea of living off campus. Moreover, dormitories, or residence halls, obviously make the campus a "lived-in" place—a place where students can be found day or night, weekday or weekend. Probably a highly residential campus will mean more chances and places for you to meet other students, even if you yourself live away from campus.

Similarly, you should determine that there is a good supply of *off-campus* housing. Once you become serious about a college or university, you will also want to find out whether the off-campus housing is affordable and either (a) near enough so that you can walk to school or (b) close to public transportation. Living alone off campus seems lonely to some people, but those who like privacy, quiet living, and independence will probably prefer an apartment to the dormitory. Living in an apartment also assures you of being able to prepare your own meals. University dormitories and cafeterias rarely serve international food.

If you are going to be a graduate student, affordable housing on or near campus may become an important consideration. As we shall discuss in chapter 11, your workload will keep you tied to the campus for long hours.

The Climate and Physical Environment

In most cases, climate should not be a consideration in your selection of an institution of higher learning. Academic benefits are much more important, and many excellent colleges and universities are located in climates or geographical areas that may not appeal to you. Of course, if you have a health problem, you may actually need to consider such matters as temperatures and humidity; and even if not, you should be aware that the United States has considerable variety in climate zones.

Here, only the briefest guide to regional climates is possible. Figure 3-3 contains an outline map of the continental United States, with the various regions identified; these recommendations might accompany it:

- For those who like hot, dry weather: the southwestern states
- For those who want plenty of snow for skiing: Alaska, the northeastern states, or the mountain states
- For those who are used to hot, humid weather: the southeastern or south central states (although these states do have winters)
- For those who like a rainy climate: the northwestern states, especially coastal areas
- For those who enjoy temperature extremes, and particularly very cold weather: the north central states of the American interior
- For those who like places where the temperature hardly changes year-round: Hawaii, southern California, or southern Florida

Figure 3-3   Regional Map of the Continental United States

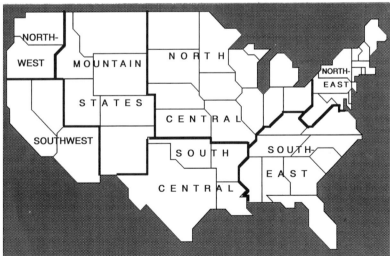

Map created by Terufumi Futaba

If you wish a more precise climate map, you might start with the free brochure *If You Want to Study in the United States: General Information,* which is available from the United States Information Service.

The geography of the United States also shows many different topographical features: mountains and deserts (particularly in the West), Great Lakes and mighty rivers (particularly in the north central states). If the physical environment is important to you, you need to study a large map of the United States and perhaps a book of nature photography.

GENERAL ACADEMIC CONSIDERATIONS

Your search for the appropriate institution will depend on whether you seek graduate, undergraduate, or English language study, but a few general recommendations are also appropriate. Remember, first, that none of these institutions is supervised by the federal government, and that even state universities and local community colleges have a great deal of autonomy. You may well ask: How, then, are standards established for higher education in the United States? And how is high quality maintained?

The answer lies in the practice of accreditation—an objective review and approval of an institution's programs by an outside agency. There are both regional accrediting associations (e.g., North Central Association of Schools and Colleges) and professional accrediting agencies (e.g., Accreditation Board for Engineering and Technology). Every five years or so, these organizations send a team of experts to visit an institution, to study its programs intensively, and to make a recommendation on continued accreditation. Colleges and universities take their accreditation very seriously, and so should you. You may check the accreditation of institutions that interest you (ESL programs excepted) in an annual publication titled *Accredited Institutions of Postsecondary Education.* This should be available at the USIS office or the Educational Advising Center nearest you. If necessary, you may order it from

Macmillan Publishing Co., Inc.
Front and Brown Streets
Riverside, NJ 08075 USA

Although a uniform accreditation guide to ESL programs is not available, you should check to see whether the programs you are considering are listed in the Institute of International Education's *English Language and Orientation Programs in the United States*. The book may be ordered from

> **IIE Books**
> **Institute of International Education**
> **809 United Nations Plaza**
> **New York, NY 10017-3580 USA**

RANKINGS

You may also wish to check various "rankings" of colleges and universities, particularly if you are interested in graduate study. These lists attempt to rate various types of programs in numerical order—the "fifty best" liberal arts colleges or engineering programs or business schools. Rankings are published both in the United States and overseas. Some must be taken seriously, but some cannot be, and all are, to a greater or lesser degree, subjective.

Your search for the best institution to attend would be easy if rankings were trustworthy, and this book could be shorter: You would simply consult a list of all the colleges, universities, and ESL programs in the United States, starting with the best and ending with the worst. Such a ranking, unfortunately, is impossible. Certainly, you want to choose schools that offer strong programs in your subject area, and we will discuss how to find these in a moment. Just now, a caution should be stated about the practice of ranking schools, because rankings can mislead you in your search for appropriate institutions.

The fact is, many applicants from other countries are overly concerned with rankings. Certain publications, in the United States and elsewhere, respond to that concern with their own ratings of colleges and universities. And not just for the schools' educational content. University sports teams are ranked; schools have been ranked on the basis of their toleration of conservative political positions; you might even see rankings of good "party schools" (that is, ratings based on social activities) or of institutions that show "Christian influence" or of those that provide the best educational bargains for their costs. These few examples should make it obvious that rankings are, in all cases, subjective, and at worst, useless.

Moreover, the criteria used in rating academic departments may be of little importance to you, particularly if you are an undergraduate applicant. The most respected rankings rate departments on the bases of faculty publications and awards, research funding received, and evaluations by faculty at other institutions. But if you are an undergraduate, you are probably more interested in excellence of teaching. In many research universities, the professors who make their departments famous may do very little teaching at the undergraduate level. In community colleges, by contrast, the faculty will attract little fame, partly *because* their first responsibility is to teach well. But good teaching is difficult to evaluate—or even to define—and so those who attempt rankings must rely on more measurable criteria.

In sum, there is no "best" school except the one that seems right for you. You might choose a top-ranked school, only to find that it fails to choose you—that is, that you are not admitted. The second one in this ranking may be too expensive for you. The third-best on the list may not offer the subject you want to study; the fourth-best may be located in a city that is too big for you (or in a town too small), or in a climate that is too humid for you. You must make your own rankings, from the factors and sources that are suggested in this chapter.

RECOMMENDATIONS IN CONSIDERING AN UNDERGRADUATE SCHOOL

If rankings are an imprecise guide, how is an undergraduate applicant to determine the worth of a prospective college or university? Naturally, the first step is to check its accreditation. In this case, regional accreditation is most important (but see the discussion of professional accreditation, in the next section). You can also take other steps to determine which institutions are academically right for you.

Of course, you must first be sure that the ones that seem attractive actually offer a degree program in the subject you wish to pursue. Many liberal arts colleges, for example, will not have an anthropology major; many business schools will not give you a degree in marketing; and even a major university with a well-regarded engineering college may not offer courses in aeronautical or ceramics engineering. Then, having determined that the major field *is* available, you must try to judge how strong the program is.

Several objective measures will provide you useful insights. First, how many students are in the department? A large department tells you two important things:

- That the department can offer a wide variety of courses

- That its program has a healthy reputation among the public

You might also ask for information on the numbers of full-time and part-time faculty and on the teacher-student ratio. A substantial number of "part-timers" suggests that the institution cannot, or does not, devote enough of its resources to teaching. A high proportion of students in relation to teachers indicates that classes will be large, reducing the amount of attention faculty can give to individual students.

Another good idea is to check the institution's catalog, to see whether the program of studies in your field is laid out; that way, you can determine distribution requirements and get a feeling for the overall education you will receive. (If the educational plan is not stated in the catalog, you may ask the admissions office to send it to you). At the back of the catalog, each course will be described, and you may find it profitable to look at that section too.

RECOMMENDATIONS IN CONSIDERING A GRADUATE PROGRAM

Applicants for graduate study need to look even more deeply than undergraduate applicants at the department's strength. Professional accreditation is very important. A business program should have the approval of the American Assembly of Collegiate Schools of Business; an architecture program, accreditation from the National Architecture Accrediting Board, and so on. Rankings are worth reviewing, assuming they have been conducted by neutral organizations, and assuming, further, that the ratings are based on faculty scholarship, library size, curriculum content, and age and size of program. Again, you should seek the advice of major professors who know the American system.

If you are a graduate applicant, try to learn, also, the amount of sponsored research going on in your field at each prospective institution. A large base of research funding does not necessarily indicate a high-quality department, but it tells you that the department has *money*. This means that it can afford today's expensive facilities and equipment—especially important considerations if you are in the sciences or an engineering field. It also means that the department may be able to offer you an assistantship or other stipend.

Meanwhile, you should be reading professional journals regularly. This too helps you in your search for a university. Who publishes in the specialized field of most interest to you? Of course you cannot choose a graduate program on the basis of the work of a single faculty member; that person may retire the year you arrive or move to another university. But if you see that several people in the department are carrying out research that interests you, you have a good reason to apply to that university.

CHOOSING AN ESL PROGRAM

> The first step, I think, he/she should do is to improve his/her English, because it can take him/her a lot of time to reach the level needed. In my country, due to the fact that it is far from the U.S., and there are no traditions of . . . relationships with the U.S., one can hardly find possibilities to study American English and to get familiar with American traditions and ways of thinking.
>
> —A student from Hungary

Choosing the right program for English as a Second Language (ESL) study also requires careful decision making. It will be stated over and over again in these pages that a high level of English proficiency is necessary if you are to meet your goals for study in the

United States—and perhaps for your career. To begin, you must master as much English as possible in your own country.

If you expect to study English in the United States, it is probably best to attend an English as a Second Language course at the college or university where you have been admitted; the reasons will be discussed in chapter 4. But you may choose not to, because of its comparative cost or your wish to see a different part of the United States (or because you want to study *only* English). We will assume, then, that you are prepared to go anywhere in the country and need help in deciding just which program is most suitable.

Here we need to discuss a guide mentioned earlier: *English Language and Orientation Programs in the United States*. This book deals solely with intensive English as a Second Language programs; the word "intensive" means that at least 20 weekly hours of instruction are offered—the minimum required by the Immigration and Naturalization Service for those international students who are studying English on a student visa. It will give you pertinent facts about costs, class size, the number of levels, the number of hours taught per week, and the duration of each teaching term.

With respect to the first of these (costs), you will find that tuition at ESL programs is usually much lower than university tuition; in fact, the ESL profession is characterized by strong competition for students, and program charges are often very reasonable. Class size is usually small—you should avoid programs where classes average more than fifteen students—and almost any responsible program will place you into an appropriate level of study (e.g., "high intermediate," "low advanced," and so on). Look also for programs that offer more than 20 hours per week of instruction as well as extra conversation classes and special activities, such as cultural outings.

Length of the "cycle" is also an important consideration for you. Some programs run for an entire semester—fifteen to sixteen weeks; others have cycles as short as four weeks. A semester's study of English can be a very tiring experience, but it is certain to be good for your mastery of the language. A four-week program, by contrast, will provide you little more than an orientation, or adjustment period, but it may be very convenient. Shorter programs may also have more skill levels (e.g., three beginning levels, three intermediate levels, etc.) and should be able to place you in a class working precisely at the level of your ability.

Finally, find out the number of students from your country in the program. Or better said, the proportion: If 70 percent of all the students come from your language background, you may have trouble speaking English outside of class.

STARTING THE PROCESS

Admission to ESL programs can take place within a few weeks, but the situation is very different for college/university admission. If you are "going to college"—a real college or university—it is probably not too soon for you to begin your research. Some experts believe that international students need *two years* to successfully complete the application process. If you expect to enroll one year from this moment, you are already behind in your work and must act quickly.

CHAPTER 4

Qualifying for Admission

THIS CHAPTER DEALS WITH THE VARIOUS PROCEDURES FOR GAINING admission to either undergraduate or graduate study in the United States. Admission into an English language program does not require our attention; usually, you will be accepted for ESL study simply by applying directly to the program, no matter what your level of English ability. Because mastery of the language is so important to college or university study, we must discuss English and ESL at various points. The emphasis, however, will be on standard procedures in U.S. college/university admissions offices.

Certain considerations apply to all applications of international students—particularly, the need to demonstrate sufficient English ability. We will examine these at the beginning, before discussing, in turn, special concerns of undergraduate and graduate applications and concluding with the practice of "conditional admission." Our first topic is a new factor in international education: agencies in your country that offer to help you gain admission.

Recruiting Agents

Usually, these companies would process all your needs to come to the United States. Of course it is much [more] expensive than [if] you do everything by yourself. Now, in my country, to study abroad is very popular, therefore many companies charge a lot. Depending on these companies may be the easiest way, but I recommend that at least they should pick ... the college at which they really want to study.

—A student from Japan

Students often ask private recruiting agents to assist them with the application process. Their action is understandable. After all, there is much information to master in making a successful application to a college or university in that large and sometimes strange country called the United States. This book would not be necessary if the application process were simple and easy, or if every country's educational system were the same as the American system.

Some agents are very efficient at handling all kinds of details, from helping you choose the right college to making the travel arrangements. Some also charge a reasonable rate for their services and have proven effective at arranging short-term exchange programs. You should understand, however, that there are two things agents cannot do:

- Although they can direct your attention to appropriate schools, agents *cannot help you gain acceptance to those schools*. Your admission will be based on your academic credentials; the agent will have no influence on the decision. The situation is somewhat different for intensive English programs, a few of which may accept students recruited by agents. But students the agent sends to ESL programs will not be able to enter colleges or universities without going through those institutions' admission procedures and meeting their academic requirements.
- Agents have no influence on the visa process. In fact, visa officers feel that students should apply for visas directly, without agents' assistance. They believe that they can give applicants all the necessary information, help them through the process, and save them a large amount of money (since agents may charge high fees).

You will also be interested to know that admissions officers in the United States have been strongly advised against making contracts with recruiting agents.

The purpose here is not to argue against the role of agents but to inform you of the viewpoint of American academic institutions. A few institutions do authorize agents to recruit students for regular college admissions, and a number of ESL programs have used agents successfully. If you have enough money, would be happy to have someone else find a suitable school, and like to have every detail arranged for you, you will probably benefit from using an agent. But choose the agency carefully. Otherwise you will do better by going to an educational advising center for assistance, by talking to students who have returned from the United States, and by making your own arrangements and decisions.

The TOEFL Examination

> This foreign language test or TOEFL is one of the most important things that will help him to be accepted. If he doesn't take this TOEFL [it] will be very difficult that the universities process his application. Moreover, the TOEFL score will help him to decide in which universities he will be accepted.
>
> —A student from Venezuela

Probably, the most important qualification for your study in undergraduate or graduate programs in the United States is English proficiency. By this time you surely know about TOEFL—the Test of English as a Foreign Language. It is the accepted measure of English proficiency for most colleges and universities in the United States and for many universities elsewhere. The TOEFL examination lasts nearly three hours and consists of three sections: Listening Comprehension, Structure and Written Expression, and Vocabulary and Reading Comprehension. The maximum score is 677, with the minimum score for admission at most colleges and universities set somewhere between 500 and 600.

You should arrange now to take the TOEFL, even if you are a year or more away from entering an American institution. It is true that certain schools in the United States are not very strict about students' English ability. An art institute or a music conservatory, for example, may waive TOEFL requirements for a gifted student. But those institutions aside, colleges and universities will routinely ask for your TOEFL score, and will deny you admission if you do not have one or if your score lies beneath their standards. Usually the required score is higher for graduate students than for undergraduates, and higher in the humanities and social sciences than in the sciences and engineering.

The format of the TOEFL—and most other tests you will take—is *multiple-choice*. That is, each section of the examination is a series of questions or statements followed by four or five responses; you have to pick the correct, or the most nearly correct, of the five. You answer by marking a small block or circle containing the letter of the response you have chosen, on a separate answer sheet. A sample of three types of questions and three styles of answer columns is shown in figure 4-1.

You may well find the multiple-choice format a strange way to measure learning; it has been much criticized in the United States too. But it has one major benefit: It can be objectively and rapidly scored, and the results can be reported to you quickly. Thus, you should expect that most standardized tests will continue to rely on multiple-choice questions, and you should familiarize yourself with them.

Figure 4-1 Sample Multiple-Choice Questions and Answer Columns

1. A word that means the opposite of *temerity* is (a) audacity (b) rashness (c) timidity (d) courtesy (e) fear.
2. *Baseball* is to *bat* as tennis is to (1) ball (2) paddle (3) rod (4) base (5) racket.
3. A major non-OPEC oil-producer is (a) Canada (b) Iran (c) Thailand (d) Japan (e) Venezuela.

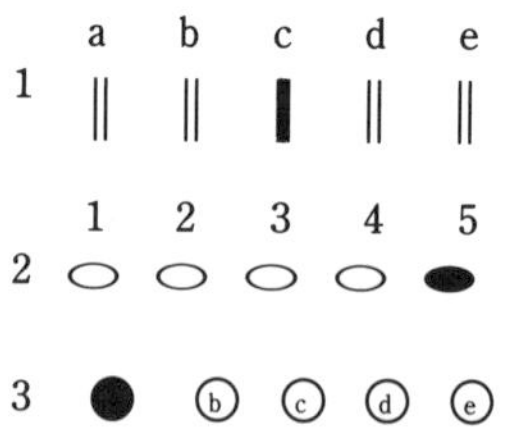

SOURCE: Bernard Feder, *The Complete Guide to Taking Tests* (Englewood Cliffs, NJ: Prentice-Hall, 1979), p. 90.

Because of the multiple-choice format, you will only mark answers—that is, make small marks on the answer sheet—on the TOEFL examination; you do not have to speak or write English. The TOEFL does not measure your ability to *produce* English, but your knowledge and understanding of the language. Nevertheless, it is difficult to study for this examination, particularly at the last moment. Sometimes students will stay up all night before the test, trying to gain enough English to "pass" it. Essentially, they waste their time. The most effective way to study for the TOEFL is to practice taking it—to learn the test-taking skills it requires. Your best advice is to go to an educational advising center or TOEFL testing center near you and to ask what TOEFL preparation materials are available; possibly a "TOEFL-Prep" course will be available as well. A list of the testing centers is found in Appendix 3. You may also order TOEFL study aids directly from

TOEFL Publications
P.O. Box 6161
Princeton, NJ 08541-6161 USA

Around the world, the TOEFL is given six times annually on Saturdays (the "International Testing Program") and another six times on Fridays (the "Special Center Testing Program"). Not every testing center offers the TOEFL six times a year, however; some offer it only once. Be sure to find out now when and where you may take it, to register well in advance, and to follow all instructions carefully.

THE TEST OF WRITTEN ENGLISH

Because TOEFL does not require students to produce English, there is now a trend toward offering a new addition to the TOEFL examination, called the Test of Written English (TWE). As its name indicates, the TWE asks students to write compositions, thus demonstrating that they can use the language. It is not currently a widespread admissions criterion. Nevertheless, you may find that one of the institutions to which you apply will require you to take it in addition to the TOEFL. You may also encounter the TWE in ESL programs, where it will be used either to place you at the right level of English study or to measure your readiness, at the end of a session, to move into the college/university academic program.

The format of the Test of Written English is very simple. You will be given a short topic to write about; the topic might require you to compare two ideas or both sides of an issue. Once you have been given your assignment, you will write silently, and without interruption, for 30 minutes. Your composition is then evaluated by trained readers, who use a six-point scale in scoring it. Each point reflects a set of criteria; thus, a "6" is awarded when your writing demonstrates such qualities as "clearly appropriate details," "consistent facility in the use of language," and "syntactic variety."

Unlike the scoring of a multiple-choice test, the grading of a composition requires subjective decisions. For this reason, your paper will be marked by at least two trained readers. Differences between the readers' evaluations are actually fairly rare, because they work closely with the criteria. But if one of two readers scores it "5" and the other "4," you are awarded a 4.5; and if they disagree by more than one point (e.g., "5" and "3"), a third, well-experienced specialist will read your paper and assign a proper score.

For more information about the Test of Written English, you may wish to order *Preparing for the Test of Written English*, written by Liz Hamp-Lyons, at this address

Newbury House Publishers
Harper & Row, Inc.
10 East 53rd Street
New York, NY 10022 USA

QUALIFYING FOR ADMISSION: UNDERGRADUATE

Your Background

Now we need to look at traditional requirements for undergraduate admission to an institution of higher learning in the United States, beginning with admission for either "new" (freshman) or "transfer" (sophomore or junior) students. Once your mastery of English has been demonstrated, your academic background counts most toward your acceptance. Because of the long American involvement in international education, admissions officers have a reasonably clear understanding of education systems in other parts of the world. They know which are the elite secondary schools in Korea or Kenya or Colombia; they have some idea of the best universities in Singapore, Saudi Arabia, and Spain. If the name of your secondary school or university is familiar to them, they will likely draw a quick conclusion about the appropriateness of your coming to their campuses.

Thus, you should expect to see a logical relationship between the sort of educational institution you have attended in your home country and the one you want to attend in the United States. If you attended a vocational or business school, rather than a secondary school that prepared you for university-level work, you probably cannot successfully apply to one of the very selective American colleges or universities; rather, you should consider schools with easier admission requirements. On the other hand, if you graduated first in your class from the most famous secondary school of your country—or finished a year at the most famous university, with high marks—many fairly selective institutions would accept you very quickly.

Your secondary school class rank is important to admissions officers. Generally, your marks need to be in the top half of your class if you are to be a successful applicant; the less well-known your school, the higher your rank should be. Admissions officers also expect the equivalent of a B grade-point average, whether you are applying as a new or a transfer student; B suggests a "good" student. Naturally, they are particularly attracted to A students.

Finally, they will look at the courses you have taken. A high mark in English literature is much more important than a similar score in an auto mechanics course—particularly in a country where English is not the first language. Whenever you have had choices of subjects, admissions officers will hope you made the tough choice, and did not take easy courses instead.

Scholastic Aptitude Test

"New" applicants—that is, those applying to enter the freshman class—must usually take a test that measures scholastic ability. Most colleges and universities require that undergraduates submit scores from the Scholastic Aptitude Test (SAT) or the American College Testing Program (ACT). These well-established examinations have proved to be good predictors of students' abilities to do college-level work. ACT, the lesser-known of the two, tests applicants' abilities at English usage, mathematics, and reading in social studies and the natural sciences.

The SATs are the most widely taken exams in the United States. They consist of three major sections with several subsections each: the Math SAT (problems in arithmetic, elementary algebra, and geometry); the Verbal SAT (questions dealing with antonyms, analogies, sentence completions, and reading comprehension); and the Test of Standard Written English, or TSWE (sentence corrections and usage). Until 1990, all SAT questions were in multiple-choice format. New versions will include questions requiring different ways of answering, but students must still be prepared to answer most questions by selecting among several choices.

The important score is the combined total of the Math and Verbal portions, which are marked along a range of 200 to 800 each. The average combined score for American students today is about 900. Competitive institutions will expect more from their own applicants—possibly including their overseas applicants. It is clear that a score of 1000 or above will be difficult for those who speak English as a second language; some institutions will expect, therefore, a high score only on the mathematics portion.

As with the TOEFL, neither the SAT nor the ACT exams can be studied for, in the way one would study for a school algebra exam. You may find that you can enroll in special "SAT prep" courses—they are common in the United States—and there are also several books on the market that claim to help students raise their SAT scores. But as one book's author admits, "Performances improve with experience" (see Donner, in "Sources"); that is, the best way to *study* for the test is to *take* the test or practice tests. That way, you will learn how to maximize your time, how to guess wisely, and other "tricks" of test-taking. Statistically, you have about a 70 percent chance of improving your score when you take the test a second time.

Begin your preparations by ordering the bulletin *Taking the SAT* from

College Board ATP
P.O. Box 6200
Princeton, NJ 08541-6200 USA

It may be helpful to read an SAT prep book as well. What will not be helpful is "cramming"—studying English and mathematics for several days and nights in a row before the test. You are unlikely to improve your score that way.

QUALIFYING AS A GRADUATE STUDENT

If you are applying as a graduate student, the qualifications are substantially more demanding. This is only natural, because a university makes a greater investment in you; in fact, your tuition—high though it may seem to you—will cover only a portion of the cost of educating you. Thus, graduate admissions committees will usually expect your TOEFL score to be higher than that of an undergraduate; your academic record, compared to that of an undergraduate, must be stronger as well as longer; you must have completed a certain set of foundation courses and performed well in them; and your qualifying examinations are different.

Occasionally, work experience is also seen as helpful. The following statement appears in *Graduate School and You* (see "Sources"):

> For some programs it is probably wise to stop after you get your bachelor's and spend some time in a job before applying to graduate school. Good work experience, positive recommendations from employers, and academic skills as demonstrated by your grade point average for the bachelor's degree are the best preparation for professional degrees. (p. 7)

Immediate enrollment in graduate programs may be more helpful than work experience, however, in fields where technology or theoretical knowledge is changing rapidly. Publications will also enhance the application of students in highly theoretical fields.

In most cases, a bachelor's degree from another country qualifies a student for consideration by a graduate program in the United States. Exceptions exist, however. Some tertiary degrees are seen as insufficient preparation for graduate work. A three-year baccalaureate program may not be recognized, for example, because Americans expect a bachelor's degree to show four years' work and the culmination of sixteen years of schooling. A change of field also causes problems; one common example is the student with a bachelor's degree in engineering technology who applies to a graduate program in engineering science. If any of these situations applies to you, you may find yourself required to complete more undergraduate courses before you are admissible.

Graduate Record Examinations

Graduate schools will almost certainly require you to take one or more standardized examinations. The best-known of these are the Graduate Record Examinations (GREs), which have both "General" and "Subject" tests. The General Test lasts about three hours and twenty minutes and consists of seven sections that alternately measure quantitative, verbal, and analytical skills. The fifteen subjects of the "Subject Tests," and their subfields are shown in table 4-1. Other well-known subject tests include the Graduate Management Aptitude Test (GMAT), Law School Admissions Test (LSAT), and Medical College Admissions Test (MCAT). All of them are in multiple-choice format, and require the student to show specialized knowledge. For such examinations, studying is helpful and, indeed, necessary.

Information about all these examinations should be available at the closest educational advising center or test center. For the GREs, you want in particular the *GRE Information Bulletin*, which contains a practice GRE (general test) and a listing of test centers. If necessary, write to

> **Graduate Record Examinations**
> **Educational Testing Service**
> **P.O. Box 6000**
> **Princeton, NJ 08541-6000 USA**

GRE Locator Services

Another reason to read the information bulletin is that you may want to take advantage of the GRE Locator Service. This new service tries to match prospective students with institutions seeking applicants who have these students' needs and qualifications. You do not have to pay for the service or even enroll for the Graduate Record Examination. You simply submit a registration form, answering several questions about your educational background and plans. This form is fastened inside the *GRE Information Bulletin* together with an envelope.

The information you submit on the form is entered into a computer. Meanwhile, institutions that wish to recruit a larger graduate student population submit data about the types of students they

Table 4-1
GRE Subject Tests and Capsule Descriptions

Subject	Subfields
Biology	Cellular and molecular biology; organismal biology; ecology, evolution, and population biology
Chemistry	Analytical chemistry; inorganic chemistry; organic chemistry; physical chemistry
Computer science	Software systems and methodology; computer organization and architecture; theory; mathematical background; advanced topics
Economics	Microeconomics; macroeconomics; finance, money, and banking; quantitative economics; trade
Education	Educational goals; school administration and supervision; curriculum; teaching-learning; evaluation and research
Engineering	Mechanics; transfer and rate mechanisms; electrical and electronic circuits; thermodynamics; properties of materials
Geology	Stratigraphy and related topics; structural geology and geophysics; mineralogy and related topics
History	European and American history, Middle Ages–present
Literature in English	English and American literature; the Bible; foreign literature in translation; literary techniques and style
Mathematics	Calculus; abstract algebra; linear algebra; real analysis
Music	Theory; history (medieval, baroque, classical, 20th century)
Physics	Classical mechanics; electromagnetism; atomic physics; physical optics and wave phenomena; quantum mechanics; thermodynamics and statistical mechanics; special relativity; laboratory methods
Political science	U.S. government; comparative political systems; political theory and history of political thought; international relations; methodology
Psychology	Experimental/natural science topics (learning, language, memory, et al.); social/social science topics (abnormal, developmental, personality, et al.); general (history, applied psychology, measurement, research designs, statistics)
Sociology	Methodology and statistics; general theory; demography and urban/rural sociology; social psychology; social stratification; complex organizations; family and gender roles; race and ethnic relations; deviance and social control; social institutions; social change

SOURCE: Adapted from the *GRE Information Bulletin, 1990–91*, pp. 26–28.

seek. Five times a year, the files are searched to determine if there is a "match." It is possible that no graduate school will be looking for someone with your characteristics, but if you answer the background questions carefully, you will likely be contacted by at least one institution.

This is not the only, or the best, way to find a graduate program, of course. As noted earlier, you should be able to pick out the programs that are best suited to your needs and interests. But sometimes you will make mistakes and overlook a promising institution. The GRE Locator Service provides you additional options.

The Test of Spoken English

If you are a prospective graduate student, you may wish to apply for a teaching assistantship to help finance your studies. The teaching assistantship will be described more fully in chapter 6; at this point, you need to understand only that, obviously, the position would require you to carry out instructional functions. Because all teachers in the United States must be able to communicate effectively in English, the universities to which you apply may require you to take an examination called "Test of Spoken English" (TSE).

Figure 4-2   Preparing for the SPEAK Test *(Photo by Stephen Barnes)*

If you are already in the United States, you will be asked to take a version of the TSE called "SPEAK," for "Speaking Proficiency English Assessment Kit."

Like the TWE, the TSE or SPEAK is quite different from the standardized tests we have described. It is entirely oral: You listen to a tape as you follow along in a test booklet, and speak when asked to do so. Different sections (seven, in all) of the test will ask you to read aloud, to respond to questions, to create a story from a series of pictures, and to discuss a world problem. The test takes about twenty minutes. It is scored by a trained linguist, who measures your fluency, pronunciation, grammar, and "overall comprehensibility."

A university will usually expect a score of 200+ out of a possible 300 for a teaching assistant appointment. Note that this is *not* a requirement for the graduate admissions office, which uses the TOEFL score as its standard, rather than the TSE. You should know also that the TSE has a comparatively high examination fee, because it is difficult to administer and score; currently the charge is US$100 (US$75 for prospective teaching and research assistants). Register to take it only if you are instructed to do so by the universities to which you apply.

Although its use is spreading, the TSE is currently administered in fewer test centers than is the TOEFL. It is also given less frequently. For example, it may be offered once annually in a test center that administers the TOEFL three or more times each year. Current TSE examination sites are included with TOEFL sites in Appendix 3. To be certain of test centers and dates, however, you should review the "TOEFL and TSE Test Center Reference List" at your educational advising center, or order it from

TOEFL/TSE Services
P.O. Box 6151
Princeton, NJ 08541-6151 USA

CONDITIONAL ADMISSION

A common practice in American higher education today is to offer international students conditional or provisional admission, pending improvement of their English skills. That is, well-qualified students—either graduate or undergraduate—are admitted to the institution on the basis of their academic credentials. But they cannot begin full-time academic coursework until they have raised their English ability to a sufficient level of proficiency, either by meeting the TOEFL requirement or by otherwise showing that they can succeed academically. In short, there is a middle ground between acceptance and denial that you should know about, for it may be useful to you.

Here is a typical case. For the moment, pretend that you are an undergraduate applicant with a TOEFL score of 450. International University, to which you have applied as a science major, sees that you have attended a good high school. You took difficult courses—calculus and physics—at this school, and you achieved A's and B's in them. One of your teachers has written a strong letter of recommendation for you. Academically, therefore, you look like an excellent prospect. But because the university's minimum TOEFL requirement for undergraduates is a score of 500, it cannot admit you to coursework. (In fact, if your score had been 447, the university might have denied you admission entirely.)

The admissions office decides to take a chance on you, and so you are accepted on the condition that you raise your TOEFL score to 500. Probably, an international admissions counselor will suggest that you take an intensive English course offered on their campus. This is not a requirement, because where and how you improve your English is your responsibility. You may be able to study English intensively in your own country, for example; perhaps the educational advising center can provide the names of local English programs. Nevertheless, you would be well advised to take the admissions office recommendation.

THE BENEFITS OF U.S. ESL PROGRAMS

First, the advantages of doing your English training in the United States (or another English-speaking country) should be very apparent. You will feel the importance of English much more strongly if you are in an environment where it must be spoken; the language changes from an academic subject to a basic necessity. Of course, studying English in the United States may seem expensive, be-

Figure 4-3   An English as a Second Language (ESL) Classroom

cause you will have to support yourself for three months, six months, or even longer, while you bring your English proficiency to the necessary level. But even students who meet TOEFL requirements often decide to enroll in a program of English as a Second Language (ESL) in the United States, for good reason.

For one thing, ESL staffs know what help you need in order to adjust to an American campus and are organized to help you meet that need. They will set up orientation programs, home stays (see chapter 8), social events where you meet Americans, and discussion groups where you can react to the new culture that you are discovering. Your teachers will probably have lived abroad and struggled, themselves, with second languages; your fellow students will be in the same situation you are in. Your classes will be small and cozy—that is, a friendly atmosphere will be established.

In fact, you should probably take the recommendation of the admissions office and enroll in the English program at "International University." The obvious benefit is that you have a chance to adjust to the location and culture of your new home before you enroll in demanding, credit-bearing courses. English language centers help you learn more than English: They help you master American life generally, and the culture of your new "hometown" in particular.

Another benefit is that you will gain a more immediate understanding of writing and reading requirements in American education. Approaches to the written text are culturally based, too; Americans have their own sense of the way words and sentences should be used together. Most college and university students do considerable writing already, and there is a trend toward *increasing* their writing requirements. The ESL staff will know your new institution's expectations for writing and reading, and will provide you the appropriate instruction and practice.

But there is still a better reason to study English with the university's own ESL staff. You have a chance to make an impression that will win their support. We will assume that, when you retake the TOEFL at the end of the course, you score only 475. But the ESL staff members are now ready to make recommendations that the admissions office accept you anyway; of course, their action must be based on the improvement you have shown in their classes. If the admissions office wants you to take more English, the ESL staff may arrange a compromise: half-time English study, half-time academic work. The Immigration and Naturalization Service will permit this situation, because two half-time enrollments add up to full-time study. But you could not arrange it if you were trying to enter "International University" while attending an ESL course elsewhere.

Delays in admission are naturally frustrating, even if you are allowed into two or three academic courses. You might begin to consider yourself a prisoner of the TOEFL exam. But, in fact, by continuing to attend the ESL program, you improve your chances for being admitted. Admissions counselors, like ESL teachers, want you to succeed. Continued improvement in English, together with solid grades in your part-time academic coursework, are a convincing argument for admission to full-time status.

SUMMARY

In some cases, then, you *can* influence the admissions decision. Clearly, you must show a certain academic promise and you must have sufficient English to open the admissions door at least a small way. The rest is a matter of preparing carefully and meeting each requirement as it comes along.

PART II

THE APPLICATION PROCESS

CHAPTER 5

APPLYING FOR ADMISSION

IN MANY RESPECTS, THE APPLICATION PROCESS IS MUCH THE SAME whether you are an undergraduate or a graduate student. In both cases, it takes a great deal of time—a year and more, from your preliminary research to your first acceptance. You have documents to gather, tests to take, statements to write, deadlines to meet, and costs to bear. It is an expensive process, because you must apply to several institutions to be sure of being admitted into one of them, and almost all American colleges and universities charge application fees.

In other important respects, the graduate and undergraduate application processes differ substantially. The financial pictures are different: Graduate school tuition is usually much higher, but on the other hand, students have more opportunity of receiving financial assistance. The tests to be taken are different, except for the TOEFL. And the faculty of the academic departments are much more involved in the graduate student application process than they are in the undergraduate process. After reviewing the common procedures, therefore, we will consider undergraduate and graduate applications separately.

REQUESTING THE APPLICATION PACKET

By carrying out the research discussed in chapter 3, you should now have discovered several colleges and universities that seem attractive to you. What you cannot do at this point is settle on one that you simply *must* attend, to the exclusion of all others. The selection process is too complicated for that. The one you have chosen, in short, may not accept you. Thus, you begin by picking seven to nine institutions that look attractive, based on the various criteria you have considered.

The best strategy at this point would be to visit each school—but such visits seem a bit impractical for you. Accordingly, you will request admission packets from all of them. Your letter should be carefully written (because it will be kept by the admissions office); perhaps the local educational advising center can provide you a model. Be sure to write your name exactly as it is in your passport and in other documents, and to write it that way in every piece of correspondence. Each admissions office, as well as the American consulate and the Immigration and Naturalization Service, will enter your name in a computer; if the spelling or order of your name is written differently in different documents, the computer may not be able to find you later.

Your letter can be of two types. The first (we will call it "Type A") is simply a request for the application packet, the financial aid application (if needed), and all current general information; see figure 5-1 for an example. Since you cannot visit the campus, you might also ask the admissions office to send you the names and addresses of students from your country who have attended that school. Perhaps there are none, or the admissions person cannot find them—it is useful for you to know such things—but if the school has alumni living near you, you have an excellent source of information to help you make your decision. You might also ask if any representative of the college will be visiting your country in the near future; if so, you should request an interview.

Figure 5-1: "Type A" Letter

Your exact address
Date

Admissions Office
International University
Street Address
City, State ZIP Code USA

Dear International Admissions Officer,

I wish to receive application material for the graduate program in Mechanical Engineering at International University. I hold a Bachelor of Science degree in Mechanical Engineering from X University in my country.

Please send me the application form, the financial aid application, and all general information about the Master's program. I would appreciate having the names and addresses of any recent graduates from this program who live in my city. Please tell me also if any representative of the university will be visiting my country in the near future, and how I might meet with that person.

Thank you for your assistance.

Sincerely yours,

(Signature)

Your name, typewritten
(Exactly as it will
appear on all official
documents)

THE INFORMATION LETTER

> Type a paper about your major field and all of your personal information and mail it to the school which is possibly available for you to study in. Of course, some schools which feel you are not qualified will notify you directly [and] can save your money and time.
>
> —A student from Taiwan

The second type of letter ("Type B") requires more time in preparation, because you will include a great deal of information about yourself. The College Entrance Examination Board, in its publication *Entering Higher Education in the United States* (see "Sources"), recommends that you give a complete summary of your educational background (schools, grades, diplomas) and plans (field of study and degree sought), the standardized examinations you have already taken, the number of years you have studied English, and the financial support available to you. The ordering information for this booklet is

College Board Publications
Box 886
New York, NY 10101-0886 USA

Once you prepare such a letter, the same letter could be sent to all prospective institutions, but pay close attention to accuracy in content and English usage. The more care you give to its preparation, the better the impression you will make on the admissions counselors who read it.

The purpose of the Type B letter is to provide the various admissions offices an opportunity to "screen" you for an application. By reviewing your summary of your academic record, they will gain a good idea of your suitability for their schools. Thus, they can respond in two ways: (a) They can send you an application packet with a letter encouraging you to apply, *or* (b) they can send a letter suggesting that you look at other colleges and universities. The second letter should be considered a denial of admission; even if the admissions office encloses an application, do not bother to fill it out. The time you have taken in sending them an information-filled letter will now be regained, because you will know which schools to avoid applying to, as well as the schools at which your application will be welcome.

WORKING WITH THE APPLICATION PACKET

All correspondence with admissions offices should be sent by air mail. You do not need to enclose a stamped, addressed envelope when you make your request, for admissions counselors usually respond promptly on university stationery. At the least, they will send you a letter or brochure giving general information on the institution, its fields of study, the steps to be taken in applying, estimated expenses for students, and admissions deadline(s). If you have written a Type A letter (simply a request for the application), they may respond with a "pre-application" form for you to fill out, so that they can determine whether you are a proper candidate for their programs. Note again that the Type B letter will probably save you time in the long run.

After you have received an institution's published application material, make sure it answers all your questions. Standards have been developed for international student brochures by a committee called The National Liaison Committee on Foreign Student Admissions; the types of information that the committee recommends for inclusion in such brochures are reprinted in figure 5-2. Schools that provide all the recommended information should gain an advantage in your decision-making process. Once you have read each brochure, you will be able to narrow the choices slightly, from eight or ten to no more than six or seven. You do not want to apply to a large number of institutions, because preparing each application requires time and concentration.

In the end, you should apply to about five institutions to ensure admission. Ideally, three of them will have the following special characteristics:

- One will be an institution about which you feel confident of admission.

- One will be a school you think might be too selective to admit you—that is, in this case, you aim slightly higher than you think you can reach.

- One will be an institution that you believe you can afford, even if you receive no financial aid.

Figure 5-2   General Information Recommended for Publication in International Student Brochures

1. Type of school (public, private, church-affiliated, community college, undergraduate, graduate, competitiveness, etc.)

2. Exact location and size

3. Accreditations

4. Academic majors and degrees (separate undergraduate and graduate)

5. Number of years to complete each degree

6. Facilities

7. Faculty (qualifications, ratio to students, availability to students, average class size)

8. Residence halls (how housing is arranged; whether or not it is guaranteed and for how many years; whether there is special housing for foreign students; off-campus housing possibilities and costs; housing for married couples)

9. Student body (number of men and women, graduate and undergraduate students, geographic distribution of students, etc.)

10. Orientation and registration (when they take place and what is involved).

SOURCE: Gary Hoover, "What's Different about Brochures for Foreign Students?" (National Liaison Committee on Foreign Student Admissions, unpubl. ms., no date), p. 4; cited in *Highlights* 30, Ohio College Association, February 1981.

The others can be the institutions you consider most desirable, based on all the criteria that seem important to you: reputation, strength in your academic field, size, and so on.

Now you must be prepared to spend money. The application fees at American colleges and universities in the United States range from US$25 to US$100. Naturally, it pains you to send several hundred dollars to five or six universities when you can attend only one. There is no other way, however, to be certain of gaining at least one admission, and possibly, of having your choice of two or three schools. During this time you must pay, as well, registration fees for the various examinations (TOEFL, SAT, etc.) that the institutions require. Think of this money as an investment, for it will repay you handsomely if you have done your research carefully.

THE ACADEMIC CALENDAR

You will need to know the start-up dates of colleges and universities in the United States that interest you. Traditionally, the academic year begins in September and ends in June, but academic calendars vary greatly; by order of frequency, the standard calendars are as follows:

- Early semesters—one 15–16-week semester beginning in late August or early September and another in early January
- "Quarters"—four term openings per year, perhaps late September, December, March, and June, and a 10–11-week term
- "4-1-4" terms—15-week semesters broken by a one-month "mini-term," usually during January
- "Traditional semesters"—two semesters beginning in late September and late January
- "Trimesters"—three three-month terms, beginning typically in September, January, and April

More than 200 institutions follow other calendars; thus, you will need to check carefully in each institution's literature for its starting dates.

You also need to check the dates when *you* can start. Freshmen, for example, can sometimes enter a college or university only in the fall—that is, August or September. Graduate students may not be admissible in the summer. And so on.

DEADLINES

Almost every college and university has deadlines for admission applications, and these dates often fall well before your time of entering studies. March 1, for example, is a common deadline given by selective schools to freshmen seeking enrollment in September of the same year, and the deadlines in very prestigious schools may be much earlier. The reason is not that universities are slow in deciding on your qualifications. Rather, they are screening applications to find the most qualified candidates. Moreover, they are seeking various balances in their student bodies: certain percentages of men and women; a fair representation of American minority groups; the appropriate proportion of international students. In a year when there are a large number of applications, they may deny admission to some qualified students. Other applicants will be put on a waiting list, and will be accepted only if someone ahead of them turns down the offer of admission.

Information on deadlines is usually given in the directories available in your local USIS office or educational advising center. While certain institutions may be flexible enough to accept late applications, you will be wise to apply on time. Naturally, your chances will be better: If your qualifications are considered marginal, you may be accepted nonetheless, while someone with better qualifications is denied because of a late application. Some experts will urge you, in fact, to apply early. The admissions office, or admissions committee, will begin considering applications before the deadline, and will probably want to start accepting qualified candidates at an early date. Figure 5-3 suggests a general timetable to follow in the application process.

Figure 5-3   Calendar for Admissions Process

Date	Action
Enrollment (E) – 24 months	Begin research on appropriate institutions, through contact with USIS office or Educational Advising Center
E – 21 months	Determine standard examinations that must be taken
E – 18 months	Prepare for TOEFL and other examinations; choose 7–9 appropriate institutions and request catalogs and other general information
E – 15 months	Register for tests; line up sources of support and people to write letters of reference for you
E – 12 months	Take appropriate tests; apply to 5–6 institutions; order appropriate transcripts and letters of recommendation
E – 9 months	Make certain all documents and information have been sent to your institutions
E – 6 months	Review acceptances; if conditional admission awarded, make arrangements for ESL study
E – 5 months	Notify institutions of acceptance or rejection of admissions offers
E – 4 months	Make housing arrangements
E – 3 months	Submit Form I-20 to apply for visa
E – 2 months	Make travel arrangements

The application form, which will be discussed below, is only part of the package you return to the admissions office. A cover letter is appropriate; again, model letters may be available at the educational advising center, or you may use the example shown in figure 5-4. As you know, you must submit evidence of your financial support. You must also have official copies of your transcripts sent, and sometimes, copies of your diplomas or degrees. If these documents are in a language other than English, they should be translated by an authorized translator and notarized (that is, made legal by the stamp of a public official).

Figure 5-4   Sample Cover Letter, Application

Your exact address
Date

Admissions Office
International University
Street Address
City, State ZIP Code USA

Dear International Admissions Officer,

Enclosed is my application for admission as a freshman at International University together with my application for financial aid. My postal order for $25, covering the admissions fee, is attached.

The results of my SAT and TOEFL examinations will be forwarded to you by the Educational Testing Service. I have asked X Secondary School to send transcripts of my work there.

I look forward to hearing from you.

Sincerely yours,

(Signature)
Your name, typewritten
(Exactly as it will
appear on all official
documents)

Finally, all test scores must be officially reported to the admissions office. Because the tests are usually marked by agencies in the United States, this process can take time. Moreover, the registration forms for the tests may provide you only enough room to write in the names of four institutions that should receive the scores; you will need to make a special request if the scores are to be reported to other schools. In summary, then, organizing application packets for five or six colleges and universities is time-consuming. Do not expect to get them all together in a few weeks or a month or two.

The Application Form

Application forms from the institutions you have chosen will probably be attractive to the eye. You may find a color photo on the cover and, inside, statements by students praising their school. You will notice that the form is actually rather thick, and you will discover that there are several pages to complete as well as a page or more of instructions on how to complete them. The school will request a great deal of information about you. You will be advised that certain questions need not be answered, such as those relating to your ethnic origin; this advice is meant to protect students from any possibility of discrimination. But the institution needs this information too, for statistical purposes, and it would be a good idea for you to respond to each item, carefully and neatly.

Generally, the questions are straightforward and can be easily answered. Because all the information will probably go into computers, however, you may be asked to mark boxes—as on a multiple-choice test—or to find and use codes for certain information. Thus, if your major is civil engineering, the code number to be entered might be 147. The institution itself will be designated by a code number on the standard examinations you take. The instructions that come with the application form will include a guide to this coding.

The application will also ask you to supply information on previous schools, jobs, or other experiences. Note that the answers are sometimes expected in *reverse chronological order*—that is, the most recent school or job is to be listed first. Finally, you will be asked to sign the application, and your signature certifies two things: (1) that you have read statements concerning your rights to the information you have provided; and (2) that what you have written is accurate and true. All in all, the application form needs to be *read* carefully first, and then completed carefully.

THE WRITING REQUIREMENT

A common feature of both graduate and undergraduate applications is that you must write a personal statement. Typically, the instructions ask you to explain your reasons for pursuing your education at the institution to which you are applying, or at least to explain why you have chosen your field of study. In some cases there is a maximum length (perhaps 100 words, or one page); in other cases there may be a *minimum* length.

Treat this requirement seriously. A writing sample will not be the sole basis for rejecting or accepting you, but it can certainly influence the admissions process. Remember that admissions counselors (or, at graduate level, departmental admissions committees) have read hundreds and perhaps thousands of these statements. Ungrammatical English will offend some of these readers, and unreadable handwriting will offend them all. They can also spot clichés, flattery, and careless thinking. It is important that you write both honestly and neatly—and that *you* do the writing; do not employ an ''agent'' to write something for you.

Spend time preparing your statement. Jot down the things you want to say and then organize them. Write a first draft, edit it, and write it again. When you have the words right, copy your statement carefully onto the application. If possible, type the statement, proofread the final version, and correct any errors neatly.

THE APPLICATION PROCESS
Transfer Students

As noted in chapter 4, undergraduate applicants are divided into two categories: transfer students and first-year students, or freshmen. The application form for the two categories may be the same. A sample application is provided in Appendix 4.

Transfer students are those who leave institutions in their own countries after one or two years of higher education and enter American colleges and universities. Naturally, these students will already have earned some credits toward an American undergraduate degree.

If you are a potential transfer student, the time required for you to complete the transfer application process may be longer than that for freshmen, but fortunately the deadline is usually later. A transcript of your previous work must be received and evaluated by the college, and an award of credits must be made—a process that often brings delays. On the other hand, SAT scores may not be required: If you have gone to a well-regarded school and have received high marks, those will probably be the basis of your acceptance.

When you receive the school's evaluation of your previous coursework, you should study it carefully; your transfer evaluation can be appealed, if you believe you deserved more credits than you were awarded. Keep in mind, also, the difference between semester and quarter credits. At an institution on the semester (15–16 week) system, students need about 120 to 128 credits to graduate; at a school on the quarter (10–11 week) system, about 180 to 190. Thus, if you receive 60 transfer credits on the basis of your work at your present school, you could be either halfway to your degree or only one-third of the way. (Note: This does *not* mean that schools on the quarter system will recognize fewer of your transfer courses; they must simply award you more credits for each.)

Usually, an institution will also have a *residency requirement*. That is, it expects transfer students to take a wide variety of its own courses—including most of the courses in the major field—and spend several terms studying on its campus. The philosophy behind this requirement is that a graduate from "International University" should have a recognizable International University education. Thus, you could not transfer 105 semester credits into International University and expect to graduate upon the completion of only 15 more. More likely, you will need 30, 50, or even 75 credits in residence to complete your degree requirements.

Freshman Admission

If you are applying as a freshman, the admissions office needs to determine your ability to do university work. A transfer student or graduate student has proven this ability at other colleges; you have only a secondary school record. Besides, you are younger, and the admissions office must be sure you can adjust to a new culture as well as to a more demanding academic environment. Thus, your secondary school record must be strong and you must demonstrate ability on the SAT exams.

Usually, you must also have twelve years of schooling— equivalent to the American primary/secondary school system—in order to be accepted for study. On the other hand, some universities have an "early admission" policy for gifted students, who may be admitted after their junior year in high school (or their eleventh year of study). If you believe you qualify for such a program, you will need to start the application process even earlier than everyone else. Incidentally, the word "gifted" implies nativelike proficiency in English.

An "early decision" policy is also common. Let us say that you know precisely the college or university where you wish to study and feel certain that you meet the conditions of admission. Thus, you apply perhaps ten months before your enrollment (depending on the institution's instructions) and ask for a decision on your admission to be made promptly. The admissions office will in fact act quickly, and you will benefit by avoiding the anxiety of waiting for various institutions to respond. Applicants who apply just at the deadline learn of their acceptance for September enrollment only in April or May, whereas an "early decision" will result in your knowing by mid-December.

Even if you choose the regular application process, you will usually be notified of your status as soon as your application can be acted upon. Most institutions now practice "rolling admissions": Applications are processed as soon as they are received. Consideration will be delayed only if your file is incomplete—that is, test scores or other documents have not been submitted. If all the necessary documents are in your file, you may receive the admissions decision relatively early. At worst, you will probably learn of your admission in time to accept or refuse admission by May 1, or shortly thereafter; you should write to any institution that has not made its decision by May 15. Acceptance may mean payment of a matriculation fee, in order to reserve a place in the college or university.

The Graduate Student

Deadlines for the receipt of a graduate application may be only one or two months before the beginning of the term, although in more selective universities, it usually falls four or five months prior. Still, it is wise, and even necessary, to be ready much earlier. If you are applying for a research or teaching assistantship, for example, your entire application may have to be filed by February 1 or earlier for the following fall (September) term enrollment. Your chances for a favorable decision rise with the promptness of your application.

Perhaps the most critical part of your application for graduate school consists of your letters of recommendation. These letters are required to be confidential; that is, you should not be able to read them. In some cases, you may be asked to return the letters with the application form, but only in sealed envelopes. More often, referees—the people who write the recommendations—are asked to send the letters directly to the admissions office.

Obviously, the best referees are faculty members under whom you have studied in the past. In the words of the Council of Graduate Schools (*Graduate School and You*, "Sources"):

> Letters from faculty members are very important because your teachers are in the best position to assess your ability to do advanced academic work. Obviously you will want to approach faculty members in whose classes you have done well. You want people who know you personally, hence the importance of talking with your teachers, both as you take their classes and when you seek advice on possible graduate programs.

Other people *may* be able to supply useful letters. The referee is usually required, however, to speak of your analytical ability, intellectual capacity, experimental ability, and/or potential for independent study, among other qualities, and your teachers are generally better able than others to make these judgments. Incidentally, you should ask them to keep copies of their recommendation letters, so that later these letters can be used for other schools.

THE LETTER OF ACCEPTANCE

If you have applied carefully, to either undergraduate or graduate institutions, you will receive at least one letter of admission. Perhaps you will enjoy the pleasure of choosing among several of the institutions that interested you. Take time with this decision. Often, students simply accept the first offer of admission and make their plans, but it is wise to be patient and wait for all the responses to come. The second school to accept you may offer financial aid, or give you more transfer credits than the first, or make itself more attractive in other ways. If finances are a problem for you, review the likely costs at each prospective school one more time before making your decision.

In each acceptance letter, you should receive information about the following:

- The program to which you have been admitted and the amount of time needed to complete it
- Any conditions imposed because of limited English proficiency or an academic deficiency
- Special conditions of enrollment, such as purchasing health insurance, payment deadlines, etc.
- New forms to be completed
- Approval or disapproval of any request for financial aid

Other documents will arrive at a later time:

- The Form I-20 that you present at the American Consulate in order to obtain your visa
- The transfer credit evaluation
- Notice of special conditions of enrollment, such as purchasing health insurance, payment deadlines, etc.

It is possible (though not likely) that you will also receive your class schedule. You might prefer to choose your courses yourself—you will have a chance to do so after your arrival—but the institution may pick courses for you so that you can avoid the great rush of registration (see chapters 9 and 10). This is particularly the case for freshmen, or for any other student who has obvious requirements to meet in the first term of study.

FOLLOW-UP CONTACTS

Once you have received responses from all the institutions to which you have applied, you should notify each of them of your decision. Certainly, the one you have chosen must receive an acceptance letter (or form) from you. It would be courteous to notify the others that you have turned down their offers, and they traditionally expect you to do so by May 1 or as soon thereafter as possible. At the same time, make sure you turn down the offer of financial aid, if any is given, so that this aid can be passed to another student.

Admissions offices now routinely call American students to provide information about their schools and to answer the students' questions. Some may telephone you overseas; after all, American institutions want you and other international students to enroll. You should feel free, in turn, to call the admissions office at your chosen institution (assuming you check the difference in time and call during United States working hours, roughly 9 A.M. to 5 P.M.). That office is almost certain to have a FAX machine as well, so that you can send your questions any time of the day or night.

We will discuss other prearrival contacts with the institution in chapter 8, after we look at financial matters and the visa process. Needless to say, you will make no decision about accepting an offer of admission until you have reviewed your financial position carefully. Chapter 6 will help you make this review.

FINANCING YOUR STUDIES

Educational and government administrators support financial aid programs so that students can choose colleges that they could not otherwise afford. All students benefit when colleges increase the diversity of their enrollments. . . . Some educators claim that if a student gets only 50 percent of his or her education in the classroom, a college is more than meeting its educational objectives—the remainder of a college education comes from students associating with each other, sharing their different attitudes, interests, and perspectives.

Peterson's 1991 College Money Handbook, p. 4

EDUCATIONAL INSTITUTIONS AND GOVERNMENT WORK HARD, TODAY, TO achieve diversity in enrollments; internationalization is part of that effort. But economic hardship at many schools has made the ideal expressed in the above paragraph difficult to accomplish. Scholarships—the outright grant of money or waivers of tuition— are increasingly rare. And "financial aid" usually means loans or offers of employment, most of which are open only to U.S. citizens. Still, international students have a modest chance of receiving financial assistance, particularly at the graduate level.

We will discuss the possibilities of financial aid later in this chapter. First, we need to look at the question of your financial support from the point of view of the college or university and the American consulate.

THE ABILITY TO PAY

Your financial backing is a matter of great concern to everyone in international education. In fact, as closely as admissions officers look at your academic record, they sometimes review your ability to pay even more closely; you may find that they ask you to fill out a very detailed questionnaire on your financial resources. Then the foreign student advisor will study your financial documents before issuing a visa authorization. Finally, a visa officer at the American consulate reviews it very carefully before the visa is approved. They will take these precautions even if you are a millionaire, and even if you have a full scholarship from your employer or your government.

You may wonder why their concern arises. One reason is that, sometimes, international students become stranded—that is, they arrive in the United States ready to study but their funding is cut off. Perhaps this is because their countries break diplomatic relations with the United States and, as a consequence, money for tuition can no longer be transferred to American banks. At other times, home governments encounter financial emergencies—the value of their currencies drops against the dollar or the value of their principal export drops on the world market. And at other times, sponsors who have agreed to support students in their studies in the United States simply do not provide the money they have promised to pay.

You can imagine your unhappiness, if you were to arrive at your new institution only to find that you had no funds to pay your bills. The American government provides no assistance in such cases, and indeed, will prevent you from taking a job to support yourself. Usually, the institution has no extra funds to help you, except perhaps as a small loan. Thus, your situation could be very serious—and for that reason, every official in the admissions process makes sure that you can support yourself during your studies.

DETERMINING THE FUNDS NEEDED

> In reality, the access [to higher education] is restricted in several ways....It's *taken for granted* that you *have an important amount* of money if you expect to have university studies.
>
> —statement by a group of new international students

The university itself determines how much money international students need. The tuition and fees are published figures—usually, you will find them stated in the catalog—and constitute the starting point. The foreign student advisor will calculate, in addition, what your living expenses must be. This calculation will be made on these bases:

- The financial experiences of other international students
- The costs of dormitory rooms
- The charge of meals provided in university facilities
- A certain percentage of the total to cover entertainment, books, laundry, and other necessary costs

If you are bringing a spouse or children, the FSA must also calculate how much extra money you will need to meet their expenses.

All this information must be placed on the Form I-20, which is the entry document the FSA sends you, and which you will take to the American consulate; the Form I-20 will be discussed further in chapter 7. The FSA must then state the sources of your support: They may be either (a) personal funds, (b) funds from the school, (c) funds from another source, and/or (d) on-campus employment. The total of your support must equal the total of your needs.

Sometimes this total will seem very high. In fact, you may have the idea that the life of a student in the United States is impossibly expensive. This is a good point to remind you that great variety exists both in educational costs and in regional costs of living.

CURRENT COSTS OF U.S. COLLEGES AND UNIVERSITIES

Several agencies collect information on college costs throughout the United States and publish it for students' use. One of the best sources for you as an international student is the College Board's *College Handbook: Foreign Student Supplement.* This directory, published annually, is in the "Minimum Reference Library" (Appendix 2) and should be available at your local Educational Advising Center. In it, you will find statements of (a) tuition and fees and (b) overall living costs at more than 2000 colleges and universities.

High, low, and average costs are reported in the College Board publication, *Entering Higher Education in the United States,* mentioned in chapter 5. The latest statistics indicate that undergraduate tuition and fees at four-year institutions range from US$2900 per academic year to US$14,500. Both figures represent a small minority of institutions; the vast majority of colleges charge somewhere between US$6000 and US$12,000. No governmentally supported institution asks a tuition of more than US$10,000, and community colleges and other two-year public institutions may charge less than US$2000. Tuition and fees at private colleges and universities, on the other hand, almost always exceed US$6000.

Your chosen institutions—particularly, those that are publicly supported—may also have separate "resident" and "nonresident" tuition rates. Thus, at a state university, only persons whose permanent addresses lie within the state receive the resident rate; at a community college, the resident rate is offered only to those who live within the "community" (which may be a city, a county, or a group of counties). Naturally, international students must expect to pay nonresident tuition.

Living expenses occupy a narrower range than tuition costs, from about US$3500 to US$6400 per academic year. Total costs at four-year institutions, then, run from approximately US$10,000 to perhaps US$20,000. It should be remembered that "academic year" means nine months. Living costs for the months outside the academic year (normally, June, July, and August) should be added to your budget. You may be authorized to take employment during those months, but you cannot count on being able to support yourself through this period.

These factors may also have to be considered:

- If you are a graduate student, your tuition will be higher, and you will have more fees and research expenses to pay.
- The cost of a private apartment (as opposed to a shared apartment or a room in a residence hall) can drive your living expenses much higher.
- Travel, and particularly trips to your home country, are not included in the estimates given.
- The cost of required books may well be several hundred U.S. dollars per year.
- Living expenses for a spouse will add at least $3000 per academic year to your costs.
- English language instruction can extend the length of your study by as much as one year, and thus add substantially to your costs.

Finally, tuition and fees are usually raised at least 5 percent each year.

You will know already the amount of tuition and fees you must pay at the institutions you are considering. Perhaps you have also developed a budget. If not, you should begin preparing one now. From the information given here, and from material sent to you by the schools you have chosen, you can estimate your costs fairly well. (If you have a school's Form I-20 in hand, you can use the figure provided by the FSA.)

PERSONAL FUNDS

Now we may consider each of the four categories of support mentioned earlier. "Personal funds" means, of course, your own money (or your family's). If you are financing your own studies, you must show the foreign student advisor (and then the visa officer) that you have sufficient money for the period of your study, or at least, for the first year of your study. If you are entering an academic program that will take several years to complete, the visa officer will want to know if you have a good chance of finding the money for the later years.

The kind of evidence accepted by the consulate will vary from country to country: It may be a tax statement showing your annual income, a bank statement, a letter of support from a relative, or an "Affidavit of Support" (see the later section, "Other Sources"). Your documents should be notarized—verified by a public official; the consulate can provide notary service, if needed. Again, they will be examined very closely. For example, if you have brought a statement of a savings account that is not in your name, you will have to prove that you have access to the money in it.

Needless to say, it is important to be honest. If you do not have enough money to meet the costs of your college, university, or ESL program, the visa officer will probably discover the truth. And even if the visa officer is too easily satisfied, you yourself would be foolish to come to a strange country without enough money to meet all the expected and unexpected costs.

FUNDS FROM THE SCHOOL

Financial aid from the college or university can be divided into three categories: loans, employment, and scholarships. Usually, these are all administered through the institution's financial aid office, even if the actual money is provided by another source. Loans sufficient to cover all the costs of a college education most often come from the state or federal government, and so are available only to U.S. citizens. And in fact, most of the financial aid to U.S. undergraduates comes in the form of loans. There are many excellent students who have had to borrow money for their education, and who will spend years, after graduation, paying off their debts.

This information may surprise and disappoint you. You may have the impression that the streets in the United States are "paved with gold," and that colleges and universities must have a great many scholarships to offer. The truth is that, today, most of these institutions have trouble meeting their operating expenses. A front-page article in *The New York Times* at the turn of this decade (December 17, 1989) carried a headline reading "Raising Money Tops Agenda of Many Colleges for 1990's"; as the article explained, many colleges and universities need to bring in money from outside sources, simply to survive.

Particularly if you are an undergraduate, you need to understand that the opportunities for financial assistance from the institution are few. As *Entering Higher Education in the United States* puts it, "There is much less financial assistance available to foreign students today than in the past. Decreasing funds from outside sources have made it necessary for colleges and universities to reserve most of their scholarship funds for United States students."

Scholarships can be divided into "need" and "non-need" categories. In the former category, the largest single source is the "Basic Educational Opportunity Grant," awarded only to very needy U.S. citizens. It does you no good to be poor in another country! Consider also the words of the director of a university financial aid office, who was interviewed for this book: When he was asked what he would say to an international student who came to him for financial assistance, he replied, "Nothing. There is no financial aid for these students." But we will dig a little further and see what hope we can find.

Non-need scholarships may be available on the basis of merit (academic excellence) but they are based on a wide variety of criteria. In this category, there are a few possibilities for you. For example, about sixty institutions reserve scholarships for international freshmen; they are listed in table 6-1. Other scholarships may be available to you simply on the basis of your academic specialty, artistic or performance abilities, special achievements or hobbies, religious affiliation, or unusual athletic ability.

Table 6-1
Institutions with Scholarships for International Freshmen

International Students

Academy of the New Church, Pennsylvania
Alaska Pacific University, Alaska
Alderson-Broaddus College, West Virginia
Alfred University, New York
Alma College, Michigan
Antioch College, Ohio
Asbury College, Kentucky
Atlantic Christian College, North Carolina
Augustana College, Illinois
Augustana College, South Dakota
Bemidji State University, Minnesota
Bentley College, Massachusetts
Bethany College, Kansas
Bluffton College, Ohio
Bowling Green State University, Ohio
Caldwell College, New Jersey
California Baptist College, California
Calvin College, Michigan
Central University of Iowa, Iowa
Clarke College, Iowa
Clarkson University, New York
College of Charleston, South Carolina
College of Saint Benedict, Minnesota
College of Saint Elizabeth, New Jersey
DePauw University, Indiana
Dordt College, Iowa
Eastern Oregon State College, Oregon
Emmaus Bible College, Iowa
Freed-Hardeman College, Tennessee
George Fox College, Oregon
Huntington College, Indiana

Table 6-1 (continued)

International Students

Liberty University, Virginia
Lyndon State College, Vermont
Marymount Manhattan College, New York
Michigan Technological University, Michigan
Minnesota Bible College, Minnesota
Multnomah School of the Bible, Oregon
Nebraska Christian College, Nebraska
Northeast Missouri State University, Missouri
Northern Arizona University, Arizona
Northern Illinois University, Illinois
Northwest Missouri State University, Missouri
Northwest Nazarene College, Idaho
Oral Roberts University, Oklahoma
Ouachita Baptist University, Arkansas
Philadelphia College of Bible, Pennsylvania
Queens College, North Carolina
Roberts Wesleyan College, New York
Saint Vincent College, Pennsylvania
Scripps College, California
Southeast Missouri State University, Missouri
Spring Hill College, Alabama
Tabor College, Kansas
University of Maine/Orono, Maine
University of Mississippi, Mississippi
University of Nebraska at Kearney, Nebraska
University of Texas at San Antonio, Texas
University of Wisconsin–Green Bay, Wisconsin
Vennard College, Iowa
Viterbo College, Wisconsin
Wadhams Hall Seminary-College, New York
Webber College, Florida
Wesley College, Delaware
Western Oregon State College, Oregon
West Virginia Wesleyan College, West Virginia

This list is from **Peterson's College Money Handbook 1991.** Copyright 1990, Peterson's Guides, Inc., Princeton, N.J. Reprinted with permission.

It does you no harm, of course, to compete for any of the available scholarships. If you must find extra funds, complete each school's financial aid application form. The point is that, in most cases, you must also look for assistance elsewhere, and expect to receive it elsewhere.

OTHER SOURCES

Scholarships are more likely to be won from an organization in your hometown or country than they are to be received from your prospective college or university. The educational advising center nearest you will be the best place to seek advice. Possible sources include Rotary International, churches, corporations, labor unions, local government offices, and private associations. This is not to say that you will find many sources in your community; there may be very few, but other student applicants often do not take the trouble to do the research. Curiously enough, scholarships occasionally go unclaimed.

Another source could be a sponsor—most likely, a relative in the United States. This person should be a U.S. citizen who states a willingness to cover all your living costs in the United States, if necessary. The sponsor must fill out a form called the Affidavit of Support (I-134); a sample is shown in figure 6-1.

Occasionally, a United States citizen who is unrelated to you may serve as a sponsor. The commitment of a relative is more convincing, however, at the American consulate. Certainly, you should not ask someone whom you scarcely know to sponsor you. The foreign student advisor will *not* be your sponsor. Nor will an admissions officer, a faculty member at your new institution, a visa officer, or the people you meet at the educational advising center. They would like to help you, but they cannot, because the Affidavit of Support requires them to pay all your expenses if you prove unable to pay them yourself. Their assistance will be limited to providing the best advice they can.

ON-CAMPUS EMPLOYMENT

The final possibility for funding is employment, but only on the institution's campus. Working off-campus is strictly controlled, and can be arranged only after your arrival. Such employment must be approved by the Immigration and Naturalization Service (INS). And when you apply for permission, INS will naturally want to know

Figure 6-1   Sample Affidavit of Support (I-134) (A)

OMB No. 1115-0062

U. S. Department of Justice
Immigration and Naturalization Service

Affidavit of Support

(ANSWER ALL ITEMS: FILL IN WITH TYPEWRITER OR PRINT IN BLOCK LETTERS IN INK.)

I, _____, *residing at* _____
   (Name)   (Street and Number)

_____
   (City)   (State)   (ZIP Code if in U.S.)   (Country)

BEING DULY SWORN DEPOSE AND SAY:

1. I was born on_____ at_____
                    (Date)   (City)   (Country)

   If you are **not** a native born United States citizen, answer the following as appropriate:

   a. If a United States citizen through naturalization, give certificate of naturalization number _____

   b. If a United States citizen through parent(s) or marriage, give citizenship certificate number _____

   c. If United States citizenship was derived by some other method, attach a statement of explanation.

   d. If a lawfully admitted permanent resident of the United States, give "A" number _____

2. That I am_____years of age and have resided in the United States since (date) _____

3. That this affidavit is executed in behalf of the following person:

Name		Sex	Age
Citizen of--(Country)	Marital Status	Relationship to Deponent	
Presently resides at--(Street and Number)	(City)	(State)	(Country)

Name of spouse and children accompanying or following to join person:

Spouse	Sex	Age	Child	Sex	Age
Child	Sex	Age	Child	Sex	Age
Child	Sex	Age	Child	Sex	Age

4. That this affidavit is made by me for the purpose of assuring the United States Government that the person(s) named in item 3 will not become a public charge in the United States.

5. That I am willing and able to receive, maintain and support the person(s) named in item 3. That I am ready and willing to deposit a bond, if necessary, to guarantee that such person(s) will not become a public charge during his or her stay in the United States, or to guarantee that the above named will maintain his or her nonimmigrant status if admitted temporarily and will depart prior to the expiration of his or her authorized stay in the United States.

6. That I understand this affidavit will be binding upon me for a period of three (3) years after entry of the person(s) named in item 3 and that the information and documentation provided by me may be made available to the Secretary of Health and Human Services and the Secretary of Agriculture, who may make it available to a public assistance agency.

7. That I am employed as, or engaged in the business of _____ with _____
                                                    (Type of Business)   (Name of concern)

   at _____
       (Street and Number)   (City)   (State)   (Zip Code)

   I derive an annual income of *(if self-employed, I have attached a copy of my last income tax return or report of commercial rating concern which I certify to be true and correct to the best of my knowledge and belief. See instruction for nature of evidence of net worth to be submitted.)* $_____

   I have on deposit in savings banks in the United States $_____
   I have other personal property, the reasonable value of which is $_____

Form I-134 (Rev. 12-1-84) Y   OVER

Figure 6-1   Sample Affidavit of Support (I-134) (B)

I have stocks and bonds with the following market value, as indicated on the attached list
which I certify to be true and correct to the best of my knowledge and belief. $ _____
I have life insurance in the sum of $ _____
With a cash surrender value of $ _____
I own real estate valued at $ _____
   With mortgages or other encumbrances thereon amounting to $ _____

   Which is located at_____
                          (Street and Number)   (City)   (State)   (Zip Code)

8. That the following persons are dependent upon me for support: *(Place an "X" in the appropriate column to indicate whether the person named is **wholly** or **partially** dependent upon you for support.)*

Name of Person	Wholly Dependent	Partially Dependent	Age	Relationship to Me

9. That I have previously submitted affidavit(s) of support for the following person(s). If none, state *"None"*

Name	Date submitted

10. That I have submitted visa petition(s) to the Immigration and Naturalization Service on behalf of the following person(s). If none, state none.

Name	Relationship	Date submitted

11. *(Complete this block only if the person named in item 3 will be in the United States temporarily.)*
   That I ☐ do intend   ☐ do not   intend, to make specific contributions to the support of the person named in item 3. (*If you check "do intend", indicate the exact nature and duration of the contributions. For example, if you intend to furnish room and board, state for how long and, if money, state the amount in United States dollars and state whether it is to be given in a lump sum, weekly, or monthly, or for how long.*)

   _____
   _____
   _____

OATH OR AFFIRMATION OF DEPONENT

I acknowledge at that I have read Part III of the Instructions, Sponsor and Alien Liability, and am aware of my responsibilities as an immigrant sponsor under the Social Security Act, as amended, and the Food Stamp Act, as amended.

I swear (affirm) that I know the contents of this affidavit signed by me and the statements are true and correct.

Signature of deponent _____

Subscribed and sworn to (affirmed) before me this _____*day of* _____ *, 19* _____

at _____ *.My commission expires on* _____

Signature of Officer Administering Oath _____ *Title* _____
If affidavit prepared by other than deponent, please complete the following: I declare that this document was prepared by me at the request of the deponent and is based on all information of which I have knowledge.

_____   _____   _____
(Signature)   *(Address)*   *(Date)*

why you now need additional money, after you, the FSA, and the consulate have all certified that you had enough funds to support yourself. Moreover, immigration officers have become increasingly strict in regulating international student employment, because they have been asked to protect jobs for U.S. citizens.

Possibilities do exist for on-campus employment, because most colleges and universities need student workers. Types of jobs include lab assistants, tutors, language informants, receptionists, computer consultants, dormitory resident assistants, cafeteria helpers, library clerks, and many others. Unfortunately, a high proportion of these will probably be taken by U.S. students under what is known as the "College Work-Study Program"; that is, government funds are provided to the university for on-campus employment of full-time students. International students are not eligible for work-study arrangements.

But if you need assistance, you should certainly inquire about an on-campus job. A few institutions may offer to arrange on-campus employment in advance of your stay in the United States, because permission can be given by the FSA, without consultation with the Immigration and Naturalization Service. You should understand that the maximum number of hours you can work, if approved, will be twenty per week and the rate of pay will probably be low. On-campus employment will certainly not provide you enough money to meet all your expenses.

One other alternative may be considered. You may enroll at a "cooperative education" institution, which requires students to alternate study and relevant work experience, for pay. This is not really on-campus employment, because most of the jobs will be in industry and could, in fact, be so far from campus that you would need to find another place to live; it is recognized by the immigration authorities, however, as part of your educational program at a "co-op" school. Your degree program would require more time (usually, at undergraduate level, five years instead of four), and here again, the employment would rarely provide sufficient income to meet all, or even most, of your college expenses. The best recommendation for cooperative education is the experience it affords you, rather than the money. Cooperative education programs have proven very attractive to international students, particularly those in technical and business fields.

FUNDING FOR GRADUATE STUDENTS

> In Taiwan, the tuition is free for graduate students, and every graduate student receives $180 each month from the Ministry of Education. However, graduate schools in America adopt the high tuition policy. The credit cost varies from $100 to $700, depending on what kind of school: public or private.
>
> —A student from Taiwan

If you wish to come to the United States as a graduate student, your opportunities for financial assistance are substantially greater than the undergraduate's. You are more successful, more mature, more experienced; an investment in your education will pay greater rewards sooner and with less risk. If you have been working for a time since you received your baccalaureate, your company is a possible source of funding. In any case, you have more opportunities both from your own country and from a U.S. university.

The best-known source of graduate student funding is the teaching assistantship (TA). The position may be named differently at different institutions, and implies various roles. At the University of California/Berkeley, for example, graduate students may be teaching assistants, teaching fellows, teaching associates, acting instructors, or master teaching assistants. But the basic TA concept is widely understood and typically operates as follows:

- A promising graduate student is offered a teaching assistantship on the basis of merit—usually after one year of study, but sometimes at the beginning of studies.
- A stipend is provided that is sufficient to meet the basic cost of living—from $500 to $1000 or more per month.
- Tuition is usually waived, thus adding greatly to the worth of the assistantship.
- The TA performs 20 hours of work weekly in an instructional role, which in the first term might be limited to paper grading, laboratory setup, or

Figure 6-2 International Teaching Assistants in Training for Their Duties *(Photo by Stephen Barnes)*

> tutoring, but may eventually become course lecturing, laboratory supervision, or leadership of recitation (review) sessions; in the latter cases, the 20 hours consists of 6–9 hours of "stand-up teaching" and the remainder in preparation, meeting with students and the supervising professor, and paper marking.

Teaching assistants are, in effect, apprentices. The university benefits from the teaching assistant system because (a) it can carry out much of its instructional mission at a relatively low cost, and (b) it can make use of the experience and knowledge of people who have advanced in their fields to a middle level. The TAs benefit because they can finance their graduate education without taking out huge loans. They also gain valuable experience, by learning how to teach.

A similar source of funding for graduate students is the research assistantship (RA). In this case, the graduate assistant works for a major professor for fifteen to twenty hours weekly on a research project, receiving in return the same financial benefits as the teaching assistant (although the amounts of the stipends may be different). The research assistantship is often considered more attractive than the teaching assistantship, for two reasons: First, it is usually less time-consuming (or at least, the work can be arranged more flexibly around the RA's own class schedule); and second, research for a professor may lead the RA conveniently into a thesis or dissertation topic, or into copublication of an article with the professor. (For further discussion of research assistantships, see chapter 11, where graduate student life is reviewed.)

Less commonly, there are "administrative" or "graduate" assistantships, under which graduate students work some twenty hours per week in a dean's office, a dormitory, or another administrative situation. Least common are fellowships, which require no work at all. These are awarded—assuming they are available—only to students who have demonstrated high academic promise.

FULBRIGHT SCHOLARSHIPS

Awards for excellence or academic promise may be available from host governments or from individual institutions; no summary of such awards can be given here. But one source of funding found virtually all over the world is worth your consideration, if you have demonstrated high academic ability: the Fulbright awards. Named for an internationally minded United States senator, Fulbright awards have been given to promising graduate students in 120 countries since 1946. About 4700 grants are awarded each year worldwide.

"Graduate Studies," the third booklet in the helpful USIS series, *If You Want to Study in the United States* (see "Sources"), contains this statement:

> The Fulbright Program, founded to encourage mutual understanding between the people of the United States and other countries through academic exchange, offers awards for graduate and postgraduate scholars and researchers. Postgraduate lectureships are also available.... There are currently [1985] 36 different types of awards from travel grants to grants which cover maintenance and study costs. Applicants must apply to and be approved by appropriate agencies in the home country.

The financial benefits of the Fulbright grant are roughly equivalent to those of a teaching assistantship. But there is no work stipulation; the recipient is free to concentrate on academic coursework and research, and should be able to complete a master's or doctoral program more rapidly. Most awards are given to students in the humanities and social sciences, but students in technical fields also have the opportunity to apply.

SUMMARY

If you have sufficient personal resources to finance your studies in the United States, you are fortunate. You will certainly find it easier to obtain a visa for study in an American institution than will students without obvious resources. Still, there are words of hope for those who have limited funds. If you are concerned about finding the money to finance your studies, remember that there are colleges and universities that offer a good education at a comparatively modest cost.

Begin developing a budget immediately, and add up all the monies already available to you. Meanwhile, look for institutions that provide good educational programs at modest costs. If you will need extra support, search for it until you have exhausted all possibilities. The fact is that the search for scholarship money is an extremely competitive game. The harder you play the game, the more likely you are to win.

CHAPTER 7

ARRANGING YOUR VISA

The best way to obtain a visa for study in the United States is to have a clear idea of what you are going to do..., I mean the university where you are going to study, where you are going to live, so that they can be sure of what you are going to do during your stay ....

—A student from Ecuador

NOW YOUR DECISION HAS BEEN MADE: YOU HAVE BEEN ACCEPTED BY A college, a university, or an English as a Second Language program, and you have accepted the offer of admission. The first stage of your research is finished, but there is still work to be done. In this chapter we will take you through the next stage, which is the process of obtaining your visa. For a start, we need to review the types of visas that may be authorized by the United States consulate.

A visa is the approval, by officials from another country, of your travel to that country. It is not a document but a message stamped in your passport, which you show upon entering the new country—in this case, the United States. Your passport is, of course, your own country's permission to travel.

A BRIEF REVIEW OF STUDENT VISAS

International students come to the United States on several kinds of visas, which are best known by their code names: the B-2, the F-1, the J-1, and the M-1. The B-2 is really a tourist visa and may be used for purposes of study only in limited cases (which will be discussed below). The M-1 is for students going to "nonacademic" schools, such as trade schools. Our focus is on academic study, where the appropriate visas are occasionally the J-1, and mainly the F-1.

100

There are significant differences between the J-1 and F-1 visas that should be noted. The F-1 is simply the "student visa," for the usual, self-supporting student. The J-1 visa, by contrast, is given to "exchange visitors"—sponsored (i.e., funded) students as well as college/university staff or faculty members. It is rarely given to undergraduates unless their own governments have provided them scholarships; but in that case, they normally *must* come on a J-1 visa, which obliges them to return home for at least two years at the end of their studies. If you are sponsored by a corporation or a U.S. agency, you may be able to choose between the J-1 and the F-1, and you should explore the relative advantages of each.

The vast majority of international students—80 percent of those currently studying at U.S. institutions—come on an F-1 student visa. That visa will be our focus here. The procedures described below may resemble those followed in obtaining the J-1 or any other nonimmigrant visa, but they relate directly to the F-1 visa process.

STEP 1: THE FORM I-20

When the admissions office at a college or university accepts you for study, your name is given to the foreign student advisor. The FSA reviews your records, then issues you a document called an I-20AB ("Certificate of Eligibility for Nonimmigrant [F-1] Student Status—For Academic and Language Students"). If you have been admitted conditionally—that is, you are required to study English full time before entering the university—*two* Form I-20s may be issued: one for the institution's English program and the other for the academic program. Sometimes the FSA will simply certify, on the academic Form I-20, that you will be given the necessary language training at the school.

A copy of the Form I-20, page 1, is shown in figure 7-1. You will need to review this form carefully to make sure it is filled in appropriately. For example, your name must be spelled correctly, and the data about your educational plans (item 4) should be accurate. Note too the dates written in item 5 about the beginning and ending of your studies. The beginning date should accurately state the time you will take up studies at the college or university; if you cannot arrive by the date indicated, you will need a new I-20. The end-

Figure 7-1 Sample I-20 (A)

U.S. Department of Justice
Immigration and Naturalization Service
Please Read Instructions on Page 2

Certificate of Eligibility for Nonimmigrant (F-1) Student Status - For Academic and Language Students

OMB No. 1115-0051

Page 1

This page must be completed and signed in the U.S. by a designated school official.

1. Family Name (surname)
   First (given) name (do not enter middle name)
   Country of birth | Date of birth (mo./day/year)
   Country of citizenship | Admission number (Complete if known)

For Immigration Official Use

Visa issuing post | Date Visa issued

Reinstated, extension granted to:

2. School (school district) name
   School official to be notified of student's arrival in U.S. (Name and Title)
   School address (include zip code)
   School code (including 3-digit suffix, if any) and approval date
   ______________ 214F ______________________ approved on ______________

3. This certificate is issued to the student named above for:
   (Check and fill out as appropriate)
   a. ☐ Initial attendance at this school.
   b. ☐ Continued attendance at this school.
   c. ☐ School transfer.
      Transferred from ______________________________
   d. ☐ Use by dependents for entering the United States.
   e. ☐ Other ______________________________

4. Level of education the student is pursuing or will pursue in the United States:
   (check only one)
   a. ☐ Primary e. ☐ Master's
   b. ☐ Secondary f. ☐ Doctorate
   c. ☐ Associate g. ☐ [illegible]uage train[illegible]g
   d. ☐ Bachelor's h. ☐ Other

5. The student named above has been ac[illegible]pted [illegible] a full course of study at this school, majoring in ______________________________
   The student is expected to report to the school not later than (date) ____________ and complete studies not later than (date) ____________
   The normal length of study is ______________________________

6. ☐ English proficiency is required:
   ☐ The student has the required English proficiency.
   ☐ The student is not yet proficient, English instructions will be given at the school.
   ☐ English proficiency is not required because ______________________________
   ____

7. This school estimates the student's average costs for an academic term of ______ (up to 12) months to be:
   a. Tuition and fees $ ____________
   b. Living expenses $ ____________
   c. Expenses of dependents $ ____________
   d. Other (specify): ____________
   Total $ ____________

[illegible]is [illegible]hool ha[illegible] information sh[illegible] [illegible]ollowing as the student's means of [illegible]ort, estim[illegible]ted f[illegible]n academic term of _____ months (Use the same number of mo[illegible]ths given in item 7).
   a. Student's personal funds $ ____________
   b. Funds from this school $ ____________
      (specify type) ____________
   c. Funds from another source $ ____________
      (specify type and source) ____________
   d. On-campus employment (if any) $ ____________
   Total $ ____________

9. Remarks: ______________________________

I-20 SCHOOL

10. School Certification: I certify under penalty of perjury that all information provided above in items 1 through 8 was completed before I signed this form and is true and correct; I executed this form in the United States after review and evaluation in the United States by me or other officials of the school of the student's application, transcripts or other records of courses taken and proof of financial responsibility, which were received at the school prior to the execution of this form; the school has determined that the above named student's qualifications meet all standards for admission to the school; the student will be required to pursue a full course of study as defined by 8 CFR 214.2(f)(6); I am a designated official of the above named school and I am authorized to issue this form.

Signature of designated school official | Name of school official (print or type) | Title | Date issued | Place issued (city and state)

11. Student Certification: I have read and agreed to comply with the terms and conditions of my admission and those of any extension of stay as specified on page 2. I certify that all information provided on this form refers specifically to me and is true and correct to the best of my knowledge. I certify that I seek to enter or remain in the United States temporarily, and solely for the purpose of pursuing a full course of study at the school named on Page 1 of this form. I also authorize the named school to release any information from my records which is needed by the INS pursuant to 8 CFR 214.3(g) to determine my nonimmigrant status.

Signature of student | Name of student | Date

Signature of parent or guardian if student is under 18 | Name of parent/guardian (Print or type) | Address(city) | (State or province) | (Country) | **(Date)**

Form I-20 A-B/I-20ID (Rev 04-27-88)N

For official use only
Microfilm Index Number

ing date should be far enough in the future that you will be able to complete your studies. If you are attending an ESL program, that date might be only a few weeks or months after your arrival; if you are going to a college or university for a baccalaureate program, the ending date should be four or five years later.

Figure 7-1 Sample I-20 (B)

IF YOU NEED MORE INFORMATION CONCERNING YOUR F-1 NONIMMIGRANT STUDENT STATUS AND THE RELATING IMMIGRATION PROCEDURES, PLEASE CONTACT EITHER YOUR FOREIGN STUDENT ADVISOR ON CAMPUS OR A NEARBY IMMIGRATION AND NATURALIZATION SERVICE OFFICE.

THIS PAGE, WHEN PROPERLY ENDORSED, MAY BE USED FOR ENTRY OF THE SPOUSE AND CHILDREN OF AN F-1 STUDENT FOLLOWING TO JOIN THE STUDENT IN THE UNITED STATES OR FOR REENTRY OF THE STUDENT TO ATTEND THE SAME SCHOOL AFTER A TEMPORARY ABSENCE FROM THE UNITED STATES

For reentry of the student and/or the F-2 dependents (EACH CERTIFICATION SIGNATURE IS VALID FOR ONLY ONE YEAR.)

Signature of Designated School Official	Name of School Official (print or type)	Title	Date
Signature of Designated School Official	Name of School Official (print or type)	Title	Date
Signature of Designated School Official	Name of School Official (print or type)	Title	Date
Signature of Designated School Official	Name of School Official (print or type)	Title	Date
Signature of Designated School Official	Name of School Official (print or type)	Title	Date
Signature of Designated School Official	Name of School Official (print or type)	Title	Date

Dependent spouse and children of the F-1 student who are seeking entry/reentry to the U.S.

Name family (caps) first	Date of birth	Country of birth	Relationship to the F-1 student

Student Employment Authorization and other Records

SAMPLE

For sale by the Superintendent of Documents, U.S. Government Printing Office, Washington, D.C. 20402

The first date is important for another reason: You cannot apply for an F-1 visa more than 90 days before your expected arrival on campus. If you are ''expected to report'' at your new school not later than September 1, it does you no good to take your Form I-20 to the consulate before June 1; the visa officer will only ask you to return after that date. On the other hand, you should not wait until the last week of August to apply, for the lines of students wanting F-1 visas can grow very long in August. And if you take your I-20 in after September 1, you will not get a visa, because that I-20 has now expired. The best time (after June 1) to visit the consulate would be as soon as you have a good idea of the date you want to arrive in the United States, since the visa officer may ask you about your proposed travel plans.

At the bottom of the I-20 is a line for your signature. *Do not sign it until you have your interview at the consulate.* Signing it before you visit the consulate is likely to cause delays.

STEP 2: GATHERING YOUR DOCUMENTS

> The employees in the [consulate] wish to see that you have a good economic situation. Therefore you have to [show] them documentation [like] a bank account, check from your job, your income tax, etc.—anything to show that you do not have economic problems.
>
> —A student from Mexico

Going to a United States consulate for a student visa is a serious business. The reason is not so much that you are about to make a major change in your life, although this is true. Rather, your visit there will be *all* business—at least, if it is a consulate that interviews hundreds of prospective students each week. You do not go to the consulate to get general advice or to relax or to have a personal chat with consular officers. They have a job to do; so do you, and there is no time to lose. You must go prepared with the right documents and the right information.

First, you must have your Form I-20 when you go; without it, there is no chance of your obtaining an F-1 visa, for the consulate at this point has no record of your candidacy to study abroad. Again, it must be accurate, for errors on an I-20 will cause the consulate to reject your application; your name should be written exactly as it is in your other documents. If you find anything wrong, it must be corrected before you go to the consulate. Write immediately (or better yet, FAX a request) to the FSA, asking that the institution reissue the I-20.

The second document needed is your passport, which must be valid for at least six months longer than your intended stay in the United States. For example, if you are starting a baccalaureate program, the expiration date on your passport will ideally be more than five years in the future. And finally, you need to bring in evidence of your financial support and your English proficiency. Because the foreign student advisor has seen this evidence and accepted it, you should have no trouble; still, the visa officer will want to study it again. Try to find out in advance what financial document is most acceptable at the consulate—a tax statement, a bank statement, a bank book, the Form I-134, or a letter promising support. To understand what the visa officer is looking for, consider this statement, which is given to prospective students at the U.S. consulate in Hong Kong (Form HNK 48):

U.S.A. visa regulations require that a consul

- must require specific documentary evidence that the applicant has funds currently available sufficient to provide all expenses for the first year of study; and
- must be satisfied that . . . adequate funds will be available each continuing year from the same or other financially reliable source.

Make sure you can provide this evidence.

One other document will probably be required: a ''Supplemental Data Sheet'' (Form OF-156), which is a request by the consulate for information about yourself. It also serves as your application for an interview. It will likely be written in two languages—English and your own—but you should answer the questions in English. You may choose to pick it up at the consulate before you actually apply for the visa, to fill it out in advance, and to read through it to determine what other materials a visa officer will want to see. This precaution will help you avoid unpleasant surprises. For example, you will probably need to paste a passport picture onto this form; if you arrive at the consulate without a picture, you may have to return with one at a later time.

If you go without filling out the supplemental data form in advance, then take two extra passport pictures as well as your passport, your I-20, and your financial support document. Go early, too, for you are about to have an unusual day.

STEP 3: VISITING THE CONSULATE

What follows is a generalized picture of the visa process in operation at consulates of the United States around the world. As was noted in chapter 3, large Educational Advising Centers may have a taped phone message about the visa procedure in your country, or even a videotape showing the steps to be taken at the local consulate. You will certainly wish to get whatever specific information is available from local sources. The discussion in this chapter, however, may better explain these steps from the American point of view.

The first thing you may notice at a U.S. embassy or consulate is the high wall or fence surrounding the entire property. Then you will see a small entrance gate, with guards standing beside it. When you enter, the guards may search you, and they will ask you to walk through a metal detector. They will take your passport and compare your face with the passport photo. If you have a camera, they will ask you to leave it with them; naturally, to avoid problems, you should not be carrying a camera. When you finally get inside the compound, you may still find United States Marines guarding the doors. You will feel, in short, like you are entering a military fortress—or that you are suspected of having done something terribly wrong.

U.S. citizens too must go through these procedures, and they too feel uncomfortable about all these security checks. The consulate is not trying to frighten well-intentioned visitors, however. It only wishes to deter the terrorists who have made tight security necessary; in recent years, several diplomats have been killed in embassies and consulates. Terrorism may not be a problem in your country, but the government of the United States has decided to be especially careful in protecting its employees. Accept these procedures as a minor annoyance. You will find that the employees themselves are polite and helpful.

Once past the guards, you check in—that is, you receive and fill out the supplemental data sheet, or you turn in the completed data sheet with your passport and ask for an interview with a visa officer. In a few countries where there are huge crowds of people seeking nonimmigrant visas, you may be given an interview appointment several days later, and so you will have to return. Consulates in many countries, however, will process your application on the day you apply.

Most likely, then, you will take a seat in a room crowded with other people who are seeking student or other nonimmigrant visas to the United States. Eventually a visa officer will call your name and you will now have the interview that determines whether you get your F-1 visa.

STEP 4: THE INTERVIEW

A U.S. government officer will ask you some questions. Let me take some examples. "What's the reason you want to go to the U.S.A.?" "When you ... finish your studies, will you get back to Korea or not?" "How is your study plan in the U.S.A.?" "Do you have any relatives living in the U.S.A.?" Therefore, you had better prepare for such ... questions ahead.

—A student from Korea

Naturally, as you wait for your interview, you have become somewhat anxious. Your request is extremely important to you, and the visa officer has the power to say, "No, we cannot approve your plan to study in the United States." Besides, you may have to speak to this person through a small hole in a window or through an iron grill—again, because of security concerns. But do not let the atmosphere influence you; the interview will probably go well, for several reasons.

First, visa officers will usually try to make you feel welcome, no matter that so many barriers have been placed between you and them. They may be people from your own country; if they are from the United States, they will often speak your language. Moreover, they have no desire to reject visa applications, when the applications are properly documented, and usually they do not. Despite their close review of your credentials, they tend to approve F-1 applications about 90 percent of the time. When they reject an applicant, the reason is often because the person seems to be an unlikely prospect for serious study. An example might be an older person who has shown little interest in academic study since leaving school, or someone who seems to be most interested in "seeing the United States" or "making American friends."

The worst mistake you can make is to be untruthful or to say things you do not mean. One visa officer complained, in an interview, of students giving answers that were provided to them by their recruiting agents. That is, the agent would tell a student that a certain question had to be answered in a certain way. The visa officer could perceive when applicants were saying only what they had been told to say, and he was impatient at hearing the same response over and over. He added that sometimes, when he was only showing friendly interest, students would feel threatened and try too hard to prove their seriousness.

Other visa officers give the same advice: Answer their questions frankly and honestly. If you do not understand English very well, you cannot pretend, to a native speaker, that you are fluent. If some of your secondary school marks were low, you cannot deny facts that appear on your school records. If you did poorly on a standardized examination, you cannot explain away the results. Remember, the college or university accepted you on the basis of the same records that the visa officer is reviewing. That acceptance is what really matters—that and the fact that you have sufficient funds to support study in the United States. Moreover, you do not need to demonstrate that you have a precise educational plan. Many U.S. students begin college without knowing exactly what their majors will be; visa officers expect you to feel the same uncertainty.

Of course, you should not tell the visa officer that you are actually hoping to work in the United States or to stay there permanently. In that case, you have the wrong visa. With a student visa, you must be a student and nothing else. It is worth quoting here from the (U.S.) *Code of Federal Regulations:*

> An applicant for a nonimmigrant visa shall be presumed to be an immigrant until the consular officer is satisfied that the applicant is entitled to a nonimmigrant status. ... The burden of proof is upon the applicant to establish entitlement for nonimmigrant status and the type of nonimmigrant visa for which application is made."

The assumption made here is that you truly want to be a student, not an immigrant or a tourist.

STEP 5: THE FOLLOW-UP

Consular officers try very hard to respond rapidly to your visa request. In a few countries whose relations with the United States are poor, prospective students are obliged to wait for security checks. Elsewhere, such as in the Philippines, consulates may be always too busy to give "same-day service"; most large posts are too busy in August, and you may have to wait at least a day for your visa. But even in large posts, an application submitted in the morning may be acted upon by early afternoon, and your documents will be returned by the end of the day. And in some places, the process is completed within an hour.

Ocasionally, an application will be rejected. You will be told the reason for the rejection, which will be one of the following:

- You appear to want to immigrate to the United States, rather than to study there temporarily.
- You do not demonstrate sufficient academic ability to pursue a full-time course of study.
- You have not presented all the necessary documents.
- You seem to have too little money to support your studies.
- Your passport is invalid or otherwise not in order.

If the rejection is caused by a problem that can be remedied—for example, if you have forgotten to bring documents demonstrating your financial support—you can reapply immediately.

Most likely, your application has been approved. In this case, you will receive your passport back, with the F-1 visa stamped in it. A sample F-1 stamp is shown in figure 7-2. Note that it has a number, which will be recorded in government computers. It authorizes you either one or "multiple" entries into the United States, and permits you to stay long enough to finish your program; this period is determined from information supplied by the FSA on the Form I-20, and is usually five years for college or university study. The name of the institution also appears with the stamp.

Your documents—the I-20 and evidence of financial support—will be *stapled in a sealed envelope* to the passport. Do *not* open this envelope. It will be opened by immigration officials on your arrival.

Figure 7-2   Sample F-1 Student Visa Stamp (with I-94)

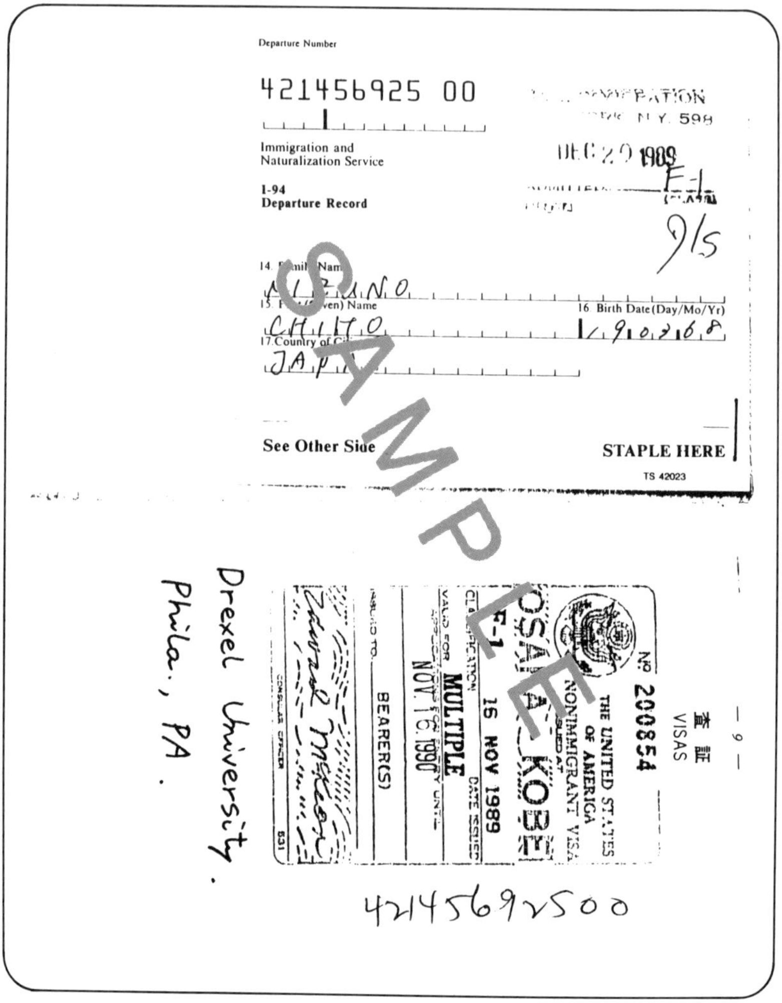

SOURCE: Provided courtesy of Chiho Mizuno

STEP 6: LEGAL ENTRY INTO THE UNITED STATES

You legally enter the United States to study only when you have a visa that allows you to study. The F-1, M-1, and J-1 are all types of "student" visas. Other visas (including some tourist visas) are not appropriate and may cause you to fail in meeting your goals. In addition, an F-1 visa is valid for study only at the school that issued you the I-20 that you used to obtain your visa. If you decide to change colleges after your arrival in the United States, you will need to request a new I-20 immediately from the FSA at the new college. Changing schools at this point is not uncommon or illegal, but you must act promptly.

Another document is necessary for legal entry into the United States. During your flight into the country, a flight attendant will give you a small piece of paper to fill out. This is the I-94, your "Arrival-Departure Record," which you will keep with you, and which will be of considerable value to you; an example can be seen in figure 7-2. At the port of entry into the United States, an officer of the U.S. Immigration and Naturalization Service will open the sealed envelope and review your I-20, your evidence of financial support, your passport, and the I-94. The officer will then write, on the I-94, the name of your institution and the length of time you may stay in the United States.

After reviewing them, the officer will return the I-94 and your other documents, including the second copy of the I-20 (the I-20B); the top copy (the I-20A) will be forwarded to your new school. A number will be written on the I-20, which is your individual number, and it will also be entered into government computers for identification purposes. Any time you travel, even inside the United States, you should carry the forms I-20B and I-94 and your passport with you.

A NOTE ON VISAS FOR ENGLISH LANGUAGE STUDY

Obtaining a visa for an English language program requires the same process that we have just described, but several differences should be noted. Some countries do not permit students to study English abroad; typically, these are countries where English is an official language and English language programs are readily available. A country may even refuse to issue passports to students who are conditionally admitted, when the condition is attendance at an English as a Second Language program. If such restrictions exist in your country, you will probably learn about them as you do your research.

Consular officers occasionally impose their own restrictions on English study—particularly when the ESL program is short and they have reason to believe an applicant will not return home afterward. On the other hand, they are usually willing to grant young people visas to study English during long school breaks. They recognize also that the financial requirements are not as heavy; they will accept evidence that you have enough money just for a short-term course. The meaning of "short-term" is understood to be four weeks or more.

In some countries, students may be issued a tourist (B-2) visa, which permits participation in an English course. The visa should be stamped "Prospective Student." This type of tourist visa is usually given to students who have not yet chosen a university or college, or who wish to travel before entering academic study. Note: If the visa officer fails to write "prospective student" on the B-2 visa, it will be very difficult for you to change later to an F-1. Again, consular staff and immigration officers expect you to know your purpose in coming to the United States and to obtain the visa appropriate to that purpose.

SUMMARY

The important points of this discussion of the visa process may be summarized as follows:

- Check your Form I-20 for accuracy, and make sure you understand its contents.
- Present it at the U.S. consulate, together with your passport and financial documents, less than 90 days but more than 30 days before your expected arrival on campus.
- Answer the visa officer's questions honestly and naturally.
- Preserve your passport with its sealed envelope of documents, exactly as you receive it from the visa officer.

Now you can turn your thoughts to arranging your trip and your arrival.

CHAPTER 8

PLANNING YOUR MOVE

Another important aspect to consider is that Americans are helpful. They are accustomed to meet people from all the countries of the world and they know that the [way of life] is different from the other countries so they are ready to help foreigners that have a lot of troubles when they come to live here.

—A student from Colombia

A NEW BUT MORE PLEASANT STATE OF PREPARATION BEGINS AT THIS POINT. You know your destination—a campus in the United States—and the date you need to be there. Buying your airline ticket is not the only thing left to do, even though you should begin gathering information about the best flights. We will consider your travel plans at a later point, and first work through arrangements for housing, temporary lodging on arrival, the transfer of money, medical insurance, and clothing, in turn. Moving to a new country may be more difficult than you realize.

Figure 8-1   Brazilian Students Preparing to Depart for the United States *(Photo by Muriel Chauvet)*

113

HOUSING ARRANGEMENTS

One of the secrets of getting off to a good start in your American adventure is to be comfortably housed. If you can arrange housing before your arrival, you will make settling in much easier, and more than that: You will be able to concentrate on your studies immediately. You have already formed a general opinion of the housing situation at your institution. Now you need to study the material sent you by the admissions office, in order to get specific ideas.

If you are a freshman, your college or university may require you to live in its own residence halls—usually, in a room with another student or in a suite of rooms with several other students—and so your decision is already made. There is good reason for such a requirement. Residence halls, or dormitories, are part of the institution's own property and are protected by its security personnel. Professional administrators will supervise dormitory operations every day and, usually, older students known as "resident assistants" will be available to provide you help in the evening hours and on the weekends. In short, universities see the residence halls as a sheltered environment for young students.

You may wish to live in the "dorms" even if you are not required to do so. Give serious consideration to this possibility if one of the following situations applies to you:

- You are making your first trip overseas.
- You have not previously lived alone or independently.
- You have no family or friends who can provide or arrange housing for you.

For convenience' sake, you may also consider enrolling in the institution's meal plan, which would typically assure you of a certain number of meals in its cafeterias at a fixed cost.

Needless to say, living in the dormitories will help you meet American students—which is, or should be, one of your goals. Sharing a rather small room with a student from the United States requires an adjustment, of course, and so does eating the food in the cafeteria; still, adjusting to the American way of life will become a necessity sooner or later. And there are several practical advantages. Most obviously, you can reserve a residence-hall room before your arrival and thus remove a major "settling-in" task. Just

Figure 8-2   Relaxing in Front of a University Residence Hall

as importantly, you can plan your budget more easily, because you will know your room and meal costs in advance. You will probably also save money, for two reasons: (1) University housing and meal charges usually compare favorably with local apartment and food costs; and (2) these services will help you avoid the mistakes we all make when we move into a new community.

There are other advantages. Most dormitories have recreation areas where you can watch television or play table tennis or other games. Kitchen facilities are often available, so that you can cook your own food. The residence halls provide you furniture, including desks; most private apartments, by contrast, are unfurnished, and you might need to spend considerable money and time in making them comfortable. Although dormitories can be noisy places when you want to study—this is perhaps their greatest drawback—you may find that the resident assistants will conduct study sessions. And finally, if you need practice with your English, you will receive constant "lessons."

LODGING ON ARRIVAL

It is also a good idea to know exactly where you will spend the first few nights after your arrival. Understandably, you may enjoy the adventure of traveling to a new city and then finding a place to stay. But it is best to save such adventures until you are familiar with the United States. If you have no family or friends who can accommodate you, or if the dormitories will not be open for move-in at the time of your arrival, expect to spend several days in hotels, and consider reserving your hotel rooms in advance. You may dislike the idea of spending the extra money, but when you are tired, the quiet comfort of a hotel is a good investment. Through careful research, you will discover the existence of inexpensive places to stay—student hostels, modestly priced hotels, or a Young Men's Christian Association (YMCA) or Young Women's Christian Association (YWCA) residence. (Note: YMCA and YWCA rooms are not restricted to Christians, despite their names.)

One alternative to a paid room is possible: Perhaps your university can arrange a stay with an American family (a "home stay") during your first few days in residence. Usually, a home stay is a short visit provided at little or no charge to you; international students often find that these visits are not only pleasant (and inexpensive), but that they may lead to lasting friendships with members of the host families. At some colleges and universities, international students can sign on for long-term home stays at a reasonable cost. If you find that these opportunities are available, write well in advance to make arrangements. People who coordinate home stays will sometimes arrange for pick-up service—that is, to meet you—at the airport, and thus provide you an additional benefit.

But even if a home stay is available, you should consider spending your first night in a hotel. A long flight is likely to leave you too tired and confused to enjoy the experience fully.

Arranging Your Finances

Well before your departure, you also need to make plans for gaining access to your funds, so that you can draw out money soon after your arrival. You will find yourself spending a great deal of money in the early days of your life on an American campus. In fact, you may spend more money during your first week in the United States than you usually spend in two or three months. Therefore, you must look into the possibilities for transferring money efficiently from your home bank to a bank in your new location.

For this reason, you should also pay any bills from the college or university before you leave—before you become temporarily "without a bank." Your tuition bill and dormitory bill probably will be sent early, and you will find due dates on them. These deadlines are likely to be strictly held: If you do not pay your debts on time, your registration or room reservation may be canceled. Thus, it is wise to settle your bills promptly, and not wait until your arrival.

Many international students recommend that you arrange to own a credit card as well. The use of credit is widespread in the United States, and in small towns as well as in cities; that is, purchases can be charged through the use of the credit card, and paid for later, when a bill of all charges is sent to you. Of course, you must choose a credit card service that is widely known in the United States.

Shortly before you leave your home country, you should also arrange to buy traveler's checks and American dollars, in order to meet immediate expenses in the United States. We will talk more about these in chapter 9.

Medical Insurance

You may be surprised to learn that you also need to consider your health, even if it is excellent now. Perhaps you are used to a health-care system where all illnesses and injuries are treated for little or no cost. In the United States, by contrast, most health care is not subsidized by the government; patients bear most of the expenses for treatment by doctors, dentists, and other health-care personnel, and this treatment is expensive. Breaking your leg, or spending a few days in the hospital because of an illness, could result in bills of thousands of dollars.

Thus, *you must purchase medical insurance.* Your institution will probably have a health clinic, but the personnel there usually provide care only for minor problems. The institution will also offer a student health insurance plan, at reasonable rates, but there might be a few days' delay in processing your application. To be safe, buy traveler's insurance to cover the duration of your trip and the first week or so of your stay on campus. But then sign up for the student health plan, which will probably give you the best coverage for its price.

The situation is more complicated if you have a "pre-existing condition"—a medical problem that has gone on for a long period of time and continues to need supervision. The student health plan may not cover the costs of such treatment. In this situation, you will need to find another insurance plan before you leave for the United States. Furthermore, if you need continuous medication, it would be wise to bring a large supply of it with you. Your medication may be much less costly in your country, and moreover, much easier to obtain. In the United States, many common medicines and drugs can be purchased only with a doctor's prescription.

The student health clinic can usually write prescriptions, but the American doctor there will naturally want to review your medical history. Thus, you should bring your medical records, written in English, whether or not you have an ongoing condition; some colleges and universities will require you to do so. All this concern for your health should not alarm you. You are a member of a very healthy age group; you will probably have no medical problems in the United States; and if you do, you will receive excellent care. But do not take chances with your health—or your finances.

BUYING CLOTHES

Should you buy clothes before your trip to the United States? Probably you will not need to if, like most students, you are beginning your studies in September. Some of the northern states may seem a little cool, some of the southern states a little hot, but often September is a month of mild, pleasant weather. If you are traveling from a warm country to any one of the northern or eastern states any time from October to March, however, you should certainly have a coat, and you might want to bring woolen clothes.

Perhaps your research shows that clothes in the United States will be much more expensive than what you are accustomed to paying at home. In that case, a good recommendation is to bring at least two changes of clothes for everyday use. When you arrive on the campus, you will probably find that you would like to wear the same kind of clothes that other students wear. Reserve some of your money, then, for North American style clothes. After you have settled into your new campus, local students can advise you where to find the best collegiate fashions and the best bargains.

Bring some of your best traditional clothing, as well, for special occasions. You may be surprised at how often you wear it. International parties, and nationality club get-togethers, may happen frequently on your campus, and the Americans you meet will be interested in your country's traditional dress. This is part of their educational experience on an internationalized campus.

PLANNING YOUR TRIP

It will be worth your while to spend considerable time exploring various travel arrangements. The costs of traveling—particularly, by air—can vary greatly, and you may find that you have a number of options. Keep in mind also that the United States is surprisingly large, so that you may need to make another long trip after your arrival at the port of entry (the city where you arrive). In such a case, it would be wise to break up your journey, and to spend a night at the port of entry before proceeding to your final destination.

Perhaps the last part of your trip will be made by bus or train, and you will need to inquire about those schedules as well as about airline schedules. Except for local lines, passenger trains are run by a federal agency called Amtrak; connections are good along the California coast, and particularly good along the East Coast, between Boston and Washington. Bus routes are more extensive; some bus companies provide nationwide service, and there are also regional companies that serve small cities and towns. You can expect your new school to provide arrival instructions; if it does not, or if the instructions are vague, write for more information.

In planning your itinerary, you should strongly consider the following suggestions:

- *Schedule your trip so that you arrive several days before the beginning of the term.* As soon as classes begin, you will become extremely busy. You need to be on campus early to settle your personal living arrangements and your finances, and to make sure you have an appropriate academic schedule. Besides, you will find that the long trip has tired you, and you will want to rest.

- *Try to arrange your flights and other trips so that you arrive at each destination in the afternoon hours.* It is probably better to avoid arriving at night or in the morning, because you will be tired and disoriented. At night, a new city is always more confusing and less friendly. If you arrive in the morning hours, you may be tempted to go to your lodging place and sleep all day, whereas you should begin adjusting your sleeping patterns to the new local time. Ideally, you will arrive at your destination in the afternoon and stay awake until nightfall.

- *Arrive at your final destination (the campus) on a weekday, during working hours.* There are many stories of international students coming to the international services office on a Saturday, needing advice or even emergency assistance—and finding that no one is there to help them. By planning carefully, you are unlikely to need help; nevertheless, it is always wise to arrive during college and university working hours (typically, 9 to 5, Monday to Friday).

  Most banks will also be closed on Saturdays. By contrast, many supermarkets, department stores, drugstores, and restaurants are open every day, sometimes until late in the evening.

Obviously, making these arrangements for travel in a distant country can be confusing, and you may want to consult a travel agent.

ARRANGING TO BE MET

Most likely, you will be traveling to a city or town where you know no one. It is appropriate, then, to notify the foreign student advisor of your arrival particulars: date and arrival time of your flight and the day of your arrival on campus. The FSA will be too busy to meet you at the airport, but at least the international services office will have a record of your arrival.

It may be possible to arrange for someone else to meet you. Arrival services are sometimes available at the major ports of entry, and particularly in New York. As mentioned earlier, a home-stay coordinator, or even the host family, may be willing to pick you up at your final destination. Moreover, large universities usually have nationality associations, some of which will meet new students. Look through the materials your new institution has sent you to see if it has a nationality association of students from your country. Even if they cannot provide pickup service, you might like to write them for advice and other kinds of assistance.

GETTING FIRST-HAND OPINIONS

Having seen to all these details, you have completed your major predeparture tasks. You can take other steps, however, to make your settling in easier. If you have learned the names of other people in your city who have studied at your school, now is a good time to talk with them. They will almost certainly be able to provide good strategies to follow.

Make another visit to the educational advising center as well. If a videotape from your new school is in the collection there, review it. Attend a predeparture orientation; in fact, you might attend several, to get different viewpoints on ways to avoid typical newcomers' mistakes and to benefit from available services. No two people have the same experience in the United States—not even if they have attended the same institution. For that matter, no two American students have the same experience or the same understanding of the problems you must solve; they might give you different, perhaps contradictory, advice. But a variety of opinions and suggestions affords you a range of tasks and possibilities—in effect, a plan.

Of course you will have your own unique experience in your new country, unlike any other person's. Listen to everyone's advice, but keep an open mind. Stereotypes about the United States—for instance, that "the American always rushes about and is too busy to help you"—usually prove false, like most stereotypes. You can form your own judgments later; just now, you need strategies for a successful trip.

In the next chapter, we will discuss that trip and the beginning of your new life.

PART III

ONCE YOU ARE THERE

CHAPTER 9

ARRIVING ON CAMPUS

*I'm surprised that every American construction [is] huge, though
I saw many pictures of the skyscraper before. First of all, when I
step into the San Francisco Airport, I feel as if I must be lost,
since I never saw such a large airport. Moreover, when I went to
New York, it is incredible that man can build such a tall
building that my head never bows down.*

—A student from Thailand

AN OVERSEAS FLIGHT IS AN ADVENTURE, EVEN FOR A TOURIST. FOR YOU,
as a new, long-term resident of the United States—and one who
will undertake the serious business of being a student in an American
institution of higher education—there are additional considerations.
In this chapter, a series of suggestions is made for your
flight and for your first few days on campus. Some relate to seemingly
minor matters, but they are included so that you will have
fewer problems, major *or* minor, in establishing residence in a new
country.

MOVING YOUR GOODS

Packing your luggage for a long stay in another country involves
hard choices. Of course, one or two suitcases will not hold every
item you expect to use in the United States. Eventually, it becomes
obvious that, in fact, you cannot carry everything you want to take,
and that some of your goods will have to be shipped separately.

You may be tempted to send a few boxes ahead. Unfortunately,
you risk losing them unless you have a friend or relative to accept
them. Sending them to the international services office is a poor
idea, for the foreign student advisor will have no place to store
them. Even if you send them to a dormitory where you have reserved
a room, there is a chance that the dormitory may be closed

or that your name will be unknown there. And if the boxes arrive with money due for the postage, no one is likely to accept them.

The best plan is to pack your boxes with things you will not immediately need, and have a family member send them after you have established residence. Your suitcases should contain the really important items: clothes, linens (towels and sheets), your toothbrush and other toilet articles, perhaps a few small gifts (e.g., for an American host family), and a dictionary or other special books. You should probably leave electrical appliances behind; if the electrical current in use in your country is different from the standard in the United States (120 volts, 60 cycles), you may actually save money by buying comparable appliances in your new location. Also avoid bringing unpackaged foods, plants, or large quantities of such goods as alcoholic beverages. Customs authorities at the port of entry may suspect that you are coming as a businessperson (to sell things), rather than as a student, and delays are likely.

If you are a smoker, you might leave something else behind: your cigarettes. It is not illegal to bring a few packs of cigarettes into the United States, nor is it illegal to smoke. You need to know, however, that many institutions (including universities) have banned smoking in their buildings. In brief, smoking has become unpopular on campuses in the United States, and you should be prepared for some frustration.

GETTING YOUR TRAVEL DOCUMENTS TOGETHER

The most important ''goods'' you will bring with you are the documents that guarantee your personal well-being. Carry these on your person or beside you on the plane, in a special case or a wallet. What follows is a review of the important documents, which may serve as a checklist as you get ready to board your flight.

First, make sure your passport and visa are in order, and write your passport number on a slip of paper that you will place in a different pocket, where you will have it in the event that your passport is lost. Carry a small address book as well, with addresses and phone numbers of the FSA or an international student counselor, places to stay, and any contact person you know in the United

States; you might add the number of the university security (or safety) office, which is open 24 hours a day, in case of emergencies.

Several important letters should be placed in this special wallet: your letter of acceptance, your correspondence with the FSA, confirmations of hotel reservations, notification of financial assistance, letters from sponsors, and any letters from people who can offer assistance on your arrival—a home-stay coordinator, a pickup service, a person from your own country. Insurance policies and insurance authorization cards go in beside them, as does your medical record.

Put in your various academic documents, or at least, have them handy, so that you can review them during your flight. The institution's catalog may be somewhat boring to read, but if you must still arrange your schedule, you might begin selecting your courses. If you are a transfer student, pack in your transfer evaluation. Although the evaluation is on file at the institution, you can show your copy to academic advisors as they seek to guide you in your course selection.

International students in the United States also recommend bringing an international driver's license with you. (Of course, you must know how to drive first!) Once you are in the United States, you can use the international license for 90 days, and take advantage of relatively inexpensive car rentals. For everyday use, a driver's license may or may not be of benefit to you. Owning and driving a car is expensive in the United States; although gasoline is comparatively cheap, insurance and repairs can be costly. If you are moving to a large city with good public transportation, or living on campus, driving may seem a needless luxury. In smaller communities, on the other hand, the ability to drive a car (and possession of a driver's license) may be necessary, or at least convenient.

You are beginning to have a thick folder of documents. Add to it traveler's checks—about $1200 worth. Remember to write the numbers of the checks on a slip of paper that you will keep in a separate place; in case the checks are lost, you will be able to recover your money by reporting the numbers to the agency that issued the checks. You will find that most commercial institutions in the United States, such as hotels, restaurants, airlines, and stores, will accept traveler's checks, and so you will be protected from most emergencies. Because taxi and bus drivers usually will *not* accept them, you will need to carry cash as well.

MAKING THE TRIP

Now it is time for you to board the plane. Your valuable documents are in your wallet or purse or briefcase. You will need to show some of them as you pass through the stages of your departure, and you might make one other stop, to buy U.S. dollars; you can also buy dollars at the port of entry in the United States, if you think the exchange rate there will be better. Wherever you change your money, get about $250–300, to cover meals, transportation, and miscellaneous small purchases in the first week of your stay. It is a good idea to put your cash in an inside pocket of your coat or slacks; if you would like to keep it especially safe, put it in a money belt that you can wear under your clothes.

The reason for all the precautions about your money and documents is that, in a few hours, you may not be quite the same person as you are now. Waiting at the airport, and saying goodbye to your family, you doubtless feel excited and clear-headed; you are also speaking easily in your own language, with people whose customs you understand. The long flight you are about to make will change most of these factors—including your clear-headedness. If you are coming to the United States from a country in the Americas, you will cross few time zones, and so the voyage will be no more tiring than making a long train trip on the ground. But flying east or west brings on a strange disorientation called "jet lag."

In a book by Ehret and Scanlon called *Overcoming Jet Lag* (see "Sources"), the problem is described as follows:

> After an easterly or westerly flight, the "hands" of the . . . clocks that exist within the human body begin to . . . spin as they search for a new schedule that will enable all your systems to function compatibly again. That interval of adjustment is described by scientists as a *transient state of dyschronism*. This is known commonly as jet lag and is that period of time during which the well-defined "old" body rhythms play tug-of-war with the . . . "new" body rhythms that must develop as the body adapts to a different sense of time and place. (p. 19)

It has been estimated that the human body needs an adjustment period of *one day for each time zone crossed* in order to recover fully from jet lag. New studies (like the one quoted from) have suggested ways to ease the adjustment, and you may want to look into them.

Despite your precautions, the chances are that you will suffer at least some ill effects of crossing time zones too rapidly. You will likely feel confused when you leave the plane; it will be easy for you to make mistakes. Concentrate on the basics: Have your passport handy, as well as the Arrival-Departure Record (Form I-94) that you filled out on the plane. After you clear immigration procedures, be sure that you have both documents still in your hand. Place them in an inside pocket for safekeeping, and move on to the baggage claim. Once you have your luggage, you will clear customs—that is, you will open your bags for inspection. Here you will be asked if you have "anything to declare." As long as all your goods are for your own everyday use, you may respond that you have "nothing to declare."

When you leave customs, with your bags, you will enter the airport terminal. Move rapidly toward the exit. You may feel as though you have no idea what to do next, but act as though you know exactly what to do. At large airports, there are people who look upon a "lost" foreigner as someone to take advantage of. Keep an eye on your luggage and on your wallet; if you have hand luggage or a briefcase, do not set it on the floor (or if you must put it down, keep it between your feet). Be suspicious of a stranger's offer to help. Go to the vehicle you have chosen for your trip to the hotel or city or campus and load your baggage onto it.

You are having an adventure, and you should enjoy it, but stay alert. Your attentiveness is not simply to assure the security of your money and belongings, but also to fight jet lag. Stay awake on your ride to your destination, go to your room, and take a shower to refresh yourself. If you have planned well, it will now be late afternoon. Try to stay awake until nightfall or, if possible, until your normal bedtime; this will help your body adjust to your new time zone more quickly. Begin to eat meals on "American time" too.

Remember that you will now be functioning entirely in English. You may see symbols that will help you find restrooms, the baggage area, and transportation stops, but you will not see signs in other languages (except, in some airports, Spanish). Nor will you be able to find translation services at the airport. Americans have begun to believe that everyone speaks English anyway—or should.

THE SECOND LEG OF YOUR TRIP

Three months ago, I packed my baggage and took the airline which is my first go abroad. I previously thought that people who live in the U.S. are almost giant [in] stature, only speak English, and [are] wealthy. However, after I took off, I saw not only what I expected to see but also some Oriental people and black people.

—A student from Taiwan

No matter which direction—east or west—you have flown, and no matter what time you went to sleep, you are likely to wake up very early on your first morning in the United States. Your body "believes" that it is still back in your country. Mentally, you will still experience disorientation; thus, it is not yet time for you to make any important decisions.

Assuming you have chosen to break your trip, you now face another flight or a long ride from the port of entry to your destination. The continuing effects of jet lag will make it easy for you to forget bags and to lose things. Follow the same routine as you did the day before. Enjoy the trip but be sure you know where your bags are at all times. At your destination, go straight to your lodging and again, try to stay awake until after nightfall.

Presumably, you are now in your new "hometown," and you have arrived as planned, during working hours. If you have encountered any difficulties, you may call the foreign student advisor for advice. If not, leave your questions until the next day. A brisk walk or some other form of exercise would be more useful to you in your current state of jet lag. With another good night's sleep, you can begin making decisions and get started on settling-in activities.

FINANCIAL MATTERS

Now, where do you start? If you talked to people back home who attended your American college or university, you may already know what to do. Otherwise, your logical first step is to telephone the international services office. Someone there will advise you how to take the next steps, which are to see to your banking needs and, if you have chosen to live off campus, to find an apartment. Financial matters naturally come first.

Setting up a bank account quickly is important because of the heavy expenses you will soon encounter. Moreover, "quickly" may mean a week, insofar as actually getting your money is concerned; unless you have wired money ahead to a bank or can present traveler's checks, or a cashier's check, you will have to wait at least several days before you can write personal checks on your new account. Meanwhile, you will have food and lodging expenses, university fees may come due, and you must buy books and other school supplies.

The most critical need for funds comes in renting an apartment. "Up-front" costs of renting are high. Particularly in large cities, landlords want to be sure they have your money before they allow you to take possession of an apartment. Sometimes they do not accept traveler's checks, and if they accept your personal check, they will ask you to wait until it "clears" (transfers to their account) before you move in. They may also ask for more money than you expected—typically, the first month's rent, the "last month's rent" (i.e., payment for the month after you give notice that you intend to leave the apartment), and a security deposit to cover any damage you may cause. In short, you could end up paying triple rent (and waiting several days afterward) before the landlord gives you the key.

Housing costs are the principal reason you need to bring at least $1200 in traveler's checks (which the bank will cash, if the landlord will not). If you are staying in university-arranged housing, you may need less; but if you have not already paid your bill, residence hall officials will ask you for a large deposit before you move in.

SEARCHING FOR AN APARTMENT

Living in an apartment requires the additional expenses of buying a bed, a desk, a chair, and a bookshelf. You can buy a bed that has been used for two years for $100. If you are an Oriental, using only a mattress is suitable for you. A new mattress is about $70. The total price of a desk, a chair, and a bookshelf is about $80 in a second-hand store. There are furnished apartments. But the rent is very expensive.

—A student from Korea

If you have chosen to live off campus, expect to do a lot of searching before you find the right apartment. You will be eager to move from your hotel, with its high costs, into a place of your own, but be patient. Many rooms and apartments are likely to be available near a campus, although the best of them will be taken by the day your classes begin. Rents vary greatly, and so do the sizes of apartments, their nearness to campus, their cleanliness, their access to public transportation, their peace and quiet, and so on. You should look at several before deciding which one to take. In the long run, it will be worth the extra expense of staying on a few days at your hotel, simply to make sure you have chosen wisely.

Either the international services office or another office at your college or university will have a list of available housing. At some institutions, a school official visits local apartments and approves them for listing. If such a listing exists, it is your guarantee of fair treatment, and you should look only at the approved apartments. In the absence of an approved housing list, you need to check each apartment carefully and to ask the landlord a number of questions. Most importantly, you must find out which services and furnishings the landlord provides and which you must provide. In most cases, furniture is your responsibility but the major kitchen appliances (refrigerator and stove) are the landlord's. You will have to pay your own telephone charges, but will the landlord pay for heat, water, and electricity? How often are the hallways cleaned? Will the landlord mow the grass, shovel snow, and keep the outside of the house looking nice? Who is responsible for repairs? Who are the other tenants? All of these are good questions to ask.

Naturally, your rent will be much higher if you live alone. You may be able to find a roommate by inquiring around the campus and by reading posted notices. Groups of students often share apartments or houses, and when one of the group leaves, the others will advertise for a new person, on campus bulletin boards. You may come across excellent opportunities by reading such ads. But ask the groups the same questions you would ask a landlord.

When you have decided on an apartment, you and the landlord will most likely sign a lease—that is, a contract; typically, it will require you to occupy the apartment for at least one year, and it may state certain penalties for you if you break the lease, by leaving sooner than one year. The amount of rent, the deposits you have given, and the other terms you have discussed with the landlord will be stated. Study the lease carefully; you might like to show it to someone in your school's housing office before you sign it.

SOCIAL SECURITY NUMBERS

Although U.S. citizens do not carry identification cards, they do have identification *numbers*. These are called Social Security numbers. International students may receive their own numbers by bringing their passports and Form I-94 to an office of the Social Security Administration.

Your need to apply for a number is not urgent—and in fact, the application process takes two weeks or so—but you will eventually find a Social Security number useful. For example, your new bank will ask for it; you will probably be able to arrange a checking account without it, but not other accounts (such as a savings account). Your college or university will want to assign you a "student number," which is usually the Social Security number. And you will certainly need it if you expect to find a job.

Ask the international services office for advice on how to apply. You may be able to get a letter from the school that will help you get your number easily and quickly.

VISITING THE CAMPUS

You should also give yourself a tour of the campus before the rush of term opening. Find out where the international services office is and go there. Perhaps you will have little real business to discuss there, but you may want to make sure your documents are in order. For example, if you have entered the country on a Form I-20 from another school, you *must* report to the foreign student advisor immediately. In this case, you will need to request a new I-20; you should also notify the FSA at the school that is expecting you. (You will follow the same procedure if you transfer schools later. The FSA at the old school is expected to submit a transfer report to the FSA at the new school.)

During this pre-term visit to the campus, you may need to register for your classes. Registration procedures vary so widely that it is difficult to predict what will be required of you. Depending on the institution, students register by mail, in person, or by telephone, either well before the term or just before the term, using sheets of paper or computer forms or computers themselves. Only two recommendations are worth making here: First, it is always better to register early than late (some institutions have a "late registration fee"); and second, the registrar's office is the place to get information.

Perhaps your school registered you for courses in advance of your arrival; nevertheless, you may want to speak with an academic advisor about your schedule. New international students sometimes take such problems to the admissions office. But admissions counselors are usually not the people to visit, even though you have corresponded with them: Once they have admitted you, you are no longer "their student," and they are not responsible for academic advisement. The right places are probably the following (although institutions vary in their advisement procedures):

- A dean of freshmen or director of the freshman center, for freshmen (or perhaps, at universities, an assistant dean for first-year students in the appropriate college)

- The college advising office, for undergraduate transfer students

- The departmental graduate advisor, for graduate students

Graduate students may also try to locate professors with whom they have had contact, but prior to term opening, faculty members are often away from campus. Probably, the FSA will be able to direct you to the right office.

Assuming you know which courses you will be taking, it would be a good idea to go to the bookstore and buy the assigned texts. You will also be able to purchase supplies (pens, notebooks, envelopes) and personal items. University bookstores are often more like department stores than booksellers' shops, for they carry items like

Figure 9-1   In a University Bookstore

gifts, snack foods, and even clothing. A typical university bookstore is seen in the accompanying photograph.

Once classes begin, you will find the bookstores very crowded. In fact, everyone at the university is rushed. By arriving early and visiting the campus, you can resolve some of your settling-in problems easily as well as begin adjusting to your new surroundings.

INTERNATIONAL STUDENT ORIENTATION

About the time the term begins, the international services office will probably have an orientation session for new international students. Be sure to go. There you will learn everything you need to know about living on your new campus. A full briefing can be expected on the topics we covered previously, such as health insurance and medical services, clothing, money and banking, housing, and immigration requirements. In addition, these topics will likely be discussed:

- Campus safety and security
- Academic questions and how to resolve them
- Employment and tax regulations
- University policies and procedures
- Opportunities to find your own kinds of food, or reasonable substitutes
- American social customs and family life

Of course, you will have a chance to ask questions on any topic of interest to you.

CULTURE SHOCK

Life in the United States is similar with life in Europe. The biggest difference is money. People in the United States first think about money then about everything else. I am in the United States about 7 months and my life is all right. I am happy with it, but I still like Europe much more. Friendship in the United States surprised me the most. Friends are [so] busy that they don't have time to visit each other.

—A student from Yugoslavia

You are *not,* however, truly prepared for your new life. No one can tell you how to adjust to life in the United States; you must make the adjustment through experience, and sometimes, through emotional distress. This is the way it usually happens: First, of course, you enjoy a period of excitement. You have a sense of freedom—you feel liberated from the rules and customs of your own culture and immensely interested in those of American culture. This period is sometimes called the "honeymoon" stage.

Then certain customs in the United States begin to irritate you. As an example, we will consider punctuality—the need to be "on time." Americans look at their watches frequently; they try to be on time for work, for class, for meetings, for games, for religious services, and even for certain social events. If you arrange to meet Americans for lunch at 12 but come at 12:30, you will probably find that they have either (a) left, (b) eaten without you, or (c) become very annoyed (even if they are not hungry). And if you come from a culture where being punctual is not important, you too may become irritated.

But any number of customs are possible irritants. Perhaps you are annoyed that American friendliness seems superficial; or, that you are unable to smoke without other people complaining; or, that Americans always act as though they are in a hurry; or, that the food never seems to be prepared the right way. Perhaps you do not even feel annoyed, just homesick. The reaction can set in within two weeks of your arrival or six months later, and its symptoms vary greatly. You might have trouble sleeping; you might, on the other hand, sleep too much. You might find yourself angry all the time, or depressed, or suffering from a vague physical illness. You may begin to dislike the United States and its people. This stage has been compared to a "morning after"—that is, the way one feels after having drunk too much beer the night before.

Nothing is really wrong with you; you are simply suffering culture shock. You have lost familiar signs and signals, you have discovered that some of your assumptions about human beings are incorrect, and you wish you could make sense of the United States. Then another change comes over you: Sooner or later, you begin to laugh, at yourself or at the strange things you see in American life, and at that point, you begin to recover. Soon you find yourself living, peacefully, with the same American customs that used to upset you. You have become bicultural.

A few years from now, when you return to your homeland, a similar process is likely to occur. The people back home will fail to do things the "American way"—which, to you, is now the "natural" way. Perhaps they smoke too much, and you can no longer stand the smell of cigarettes. Or they do things in a leisurely way, whereas you organize the events of your day and look constantly at your watch. So you become annoyed with *them*.

This illness is known as "reverse culture shock." Fortunately, it too is curable.

CHAPTER 10

ADJUSTING TO THE UNDERGRADUATE CLASSROOM

[The] difficulty of studying in universities or colleges surprised me so much, because it is very different from the state of universities or colleges in Japan. In Japan, students . . . do not have to study hard because generally [universities] are difficult to enter and easy to graduate [from].

—A student from Japan

NOW THAT WE HAVE DISCUSSED ADJUSTMENT TO ALL THE MOST IMMEDIATE concerns you face, it is time to say something about adjustment to the educational system. The focus in this chapter is on undergraduate classes, although many of the procedures and practices described fit the graduate classroom as well. Essentially, we will look at U.S. educational philosophy put into action; that is, the chapter is organized around characteristics of higher education in the United States that are not commonly found in universities elsewhere.

The first point to make is that the work starts quickly, and you need to be ready, with the first class, to concentrate on your studies; calendars and schedules are as important to American educators as the clock is. Possibly you will enroll in coursework on a Friday, be given assignments of homework during your first set of classes on Monday, and have to turn in at least one of your assignments by the next class meeting. In U.S. colleges and universities, the student is accountable for his or her work from the first day, and must make serious choices even before classes begin.

ADD-DROP

In the week before term begins, and in the first few days of classes, you will probably see long lines of students waiting to speak with academic advisors about their schedules. This activity is overseen by the registrar, the official who manages course enrollment, room assignments, grade reports, and all student records; the office is sometimes called, in fact, the "Office of Student Records." The students may be registering for their courses, and you may be standing there with them, doing the same. On the other hand, they may simply be adjusting their course assignments, so that their schedules become more convenient to them. The series of days in which this process takes place is known as the "add-drop" period. "Add-drop" needs some explanation, and some acceptance on your part.

A particular feature of American higher education is students' freedom to choose many of their own courses. For example, if a student has enrolled in a chemistry course to meet a science requirement, he or she may decide at the last moment to take a biology course instead. Similarly, students may suddenly decide to change their electives (the courses they choose out of their own interest); they must earn a certain number of elective credits to graduate, but otherwise, they have few restrictions on their *choice* of elective courses. They are also free to choose a different course "section" (that is, an offering of the same course at a different time and with a different instructor). In particular, students tend to avoid courses that interfere with their sleep in the morning or with their employment or social activities in the late afternoon. Thus, they will drop 8 A.M. or 4 P.M. sections and try to add sections that meet in the middle of the day.

The students' right to make these choices is recognized and accepted, despite the extra work it causes for administrators. Students can (and do) add and drop frequently in the first few days of each term, although certain restrictions are placed on their choices; for example, they must have the prerequisites (the necessary preparation classes) for the courses they request, and the requested section must be "open"—that is, the number of students already enrolled cannot exceed enrollment limits. You too will want to take advantage of the add-drop process. At the beginning, you may feel that, by rearranging your schedule, you take too much responsibility for your education into your own hands. Eventually, you will probably appreciate the freedom and flexibility add-drop allows you.

THE FIRST CLASS

You may also be surprised by the first meeting of each of your courses, because your instructors will spend most or all of their time on administrative tasks. They will give you copies of their course outlines and make sure you know the locations of their offices. They will "call the roll" (that is, check to see who is present); discuss the textbook; state their grading policies; and go through their course program in some detail. In a small class, they may ask you to introduce yourself. Perhaps the only substantive work of the hour will be a brief introduction to the topic of the next class meeting and an assignment of pages to read for it.

The reading will almost certainly be in the designated textbook. In American undergraduate classes, instructors usually do not give out bibliographies of books that the student must then find in the library. Rather, they will assign one or two books which must be purchased, and which they will follow in presenting course material. Typically, you will not need to read other books: The examinations will be based entirely on readings in the textbook(s) and the instructor's presentations.

The course outline (sometimes called the "syllabus") is your guide to the course. You should keep it in your notebook and read it occasionally during the term, particularly to be sure of test dates and special assignments; make sure, as well, that you understand each instructor's grading policies. In effect, the course outline is a contract your instructors make with you. They can, of course, change the assignments, whereas you cannot. But generally you will be able to determine fairly quickly whether the course or the instructor meets your needs and wishes, and if not, you can drop the course before the end of the add-drop period.

Once you decide to remain in your classes, you accept the instructors' control of your coursework. They will monitor your participation, inform the registrar of your standing in the course, and eventually, submit grades for you. They determine the amount of reading, the course assignments, and the number of tests. In the United States, professors expect to have this "academic freedom"—the right to decide what material to present and how to present it and to measure how well you have mastered it. They alone have the right to determine your grades.

INFORMALITY

You are not likely to be the only international student in your class, and indeed, your classmates may be from all the continents of the world. Thus, it is not likely that they will stare at you. In fact, you may wonder why they do not take *more* interest in you. Here is what a Turkish student has written:

> A lot of Americans don't [have] geographical knowledge, because I've asked them, "Where is Turkey or Italy or Greece?" They couldn't answer me. . . . Of course, the USA is a very good country . . . but they also must learn about other countries. So how about Turkish life or French life?

When you become friends with your classmates, you will probably need to educate them on "geographical knowledge."

You may also find older students taking the course with you, for many American adults are returning to college, on a part-time or full-time basis. But the majority of the class will be younger students (eighteen to twenty-two years old), among whom you will probably notice an attitude of informality. The casual atmosphere in some classrooms may be difficult, in fact, for you to adjust to. It is not necessarily the "right" educational atmosphere: It is simply a feature of American culture as it relates to higher education.

You will immediately notice informal dress: T-shirts, sweatshirts, shorts and sandals in warm weather, jeans that may or may not have holes in them. Instructors often dress with equal casualness. This is especially true if they are graduate teaching assistants, but middle-aged professors—probably, males more than females—often dress casually as well. There is a sense among faculty members in the United States that very formal dress makes them seem too authoritarian; they want students to relax, for reasons that will be addressed later.

Informality is apparent in many other ways. Students may eat their lunches while the instructor is talking; occasionally, students will sip soft drinks during class. Although it is considered somewhat impolite, instructors may drink coffee while they are conducting class. Students tip back their chairs, slouch down in their seats, whisper to each other, and look out the window. They sometimes come late—after the teacher has started the class—or leave early. They may interrupt the instructor to ask questions or make comments, in a way that would seem rude in your country. And so on.

In some cases, the American classroom is, doubtless, too informal. You may choose to dress neatly, arrive promptly for class, and address your instructors formally and respectfully; indeed, they will appreciate such behavior. But accept the fact that informality has its advantages too. Specifically, when students feel comfortable, they are able to concentrate entirely on their learning.

THE INTERACTIVE CLASSROOM

Faculty members seeking alternatives to the classroom lecture are turning in growing numbers to a strategy that transforms the traditional relationship between teachers and students.

With this strategy, known as collaborative learning, the professor no longer acts like an expert dispensing knowledge to passive students. Instead, he or she assigns the students a project, which they tackle together in small groups.

From *The Chronicle of Higher Education,*
Aug. 2, 1989, p. A9.

A feature of U.S. education that we have not yet discussed is continuous classroom interaction between teacher and students. From Los Angeles to New York, and from Chicago to Houston, educators believe that students master information by discovering it for themselves—that teachers do not actually teach, but simply help students learn. In this view, learning takes place through a process of challenging old ideas and asking questions. Because the formal lecture permits little questioning, it is less common in the United States than in many countries; as the quotation above indicates, the faculty member aims to exchange ideas with students, rather than simply tell them what they should know.

The concept of constantly exchanging ideas may seem strange to you at first. Perhaps you come from a country where people believe that whatever is written in a book must be true, and that teachers are always right in matters of learning; if so, you will probably find the United States system disquieting. Of course, American students know that their textbooks are mostly right and that their teachers are better informed than they are. But they think for themselves—and their teachers expect them to ask questions and challenge ideas. The point, again, is not that Americans have the "right" approach to learning, but that the interactive classroom is a strong feature of U.S. education. You will need to adjust to it—and in time, take advantage of it.

The accompanying picture shows a class in an English as a Second Language program, where the tradition of interactive teaching is especially strong. Note that the students are sitting in a circle, so that each of them can see every other student. They are working in pairs, interacting with each other. The teacher, at the left, is listening to one pair and giving them individual attention. The class con-

Figure 10-1   A Class in an ESL Program

tains only ten students, so that each has a chance to speak, to ask questions, and to receive the teacher's help.

Comparatively few courses in the university classroom are so clearly organized for interaction. Nevertheless, the course in which a professor lectures steadily to hundreds of silent students is relatively rare in the United States. Enrollments are often limited (many classes will have fewer than thirty students), so that all students have a chance to participate. Where the lecture format is necessary, as in a freshman chemistry course, the large class meets once or twice a week, then divides into "recitation sections," or small-group meetings. The lecture is used to present information efficiently—for example, through slides and demonstrations as well as actual lecturing—but recitations provide important sessions where homework can be reviewed and questions answered.

You will find your classmates raising their hands to ask questions (and sometimes, asking questions without raising their hands). The instructor will also ask them, and you, questions in order to check the group's understanding. All this is considered part of the learning process. If you do not understand a concept, you are expected to ask for clarification; if you *do* understand, you are expected to be able to state the concept. Be prepared for your instructors' questioning. Particularly in freshman/sophomore courses, they may base part of your grade on your efforts to participate in the work of the class. That is, you will be graded on such matters as your attendance, your promptness in arriving in class, your ability to get assignments in on time, and your interest in the course, as shown by your questions and by the answers you give to instructors' questions.

You may believe that it is impolite to ask a teacher a question, and that it is offensive to challenge a teacher's presentation (for example, to ask, "But how can we solve the equation if we are not given the value of y?"). In North American culture, however, it is impolite only to *interrupt* the teacher with a question and offensive only to *attack* the teacher's presentation (for example, to say, "How can we solve the problem if you don't present it clearly?"). Questioning—particularly, that which shows students trying to learn for themselves—is appreciated and encouraged. By contrast, memorization is considered a poor way to learn. Rewards in the form of good grades will come if you have an inquiring mind and think for yourself.

OFFICE HOURS

A continuation of the concept of interaction between teacher and student is the practice of office hours. That is, your instructors will give you hours on certain days when they will be available in their offices to speak with you. Many will offer you a chance to see them at times outside office hours, and provide you their office phone numbers to call if you want an appointment; a few will even give you their home telephone numbers. Thus, the student's ability to ask questions extends beyond the class hour.

Moreover, professors in certain courses will encourage you to attend tutorial sessions. Writing instructors will expect you to bring drafts of your papers to their offices for review and criticism, or to a writing center staffed by other teachers. A calculus instructor may ask you to see a graduate assistant for a math tutorial. Or a history professor may send you to the library for a session with a reference librarian on conducting research for a paper. These activities take the student to the logical goal of interaction: individualized instruction. That is, students and educators in the United States tend to believe that the ideal learning situation for a student is speaking alone with a teacher. In the United States, tutors are not assigned directly to courses, but clearly, much tutorial help is available; during office hours, professors become in effect tutors.

Many students, native and international, fail to take advantage of office hours. The reasons vary, from fear of the instructor's authority or embarrassment at not understanding the material, to overconfidence about their performance in the course. You should begin your education in the United States with the understanding that visiting your professors in their offices is a way to improve your performance in their classes. It is also "participation": It shows your interest in the class and your inquiring mind. In all likelihood, the instructor will appreciate your interest and will try to make you feel comfortable.

SUDDEN REQUIREMENTS

"Keeping up" is extremely important in all of your classes. It is considered crucial in mathematics, for example, to master each day's material before going to the next class, because new points often depend entirely on old points. But it has importance for other reasons in all your courses: Your grade depends upon your being prepared, not just for every examination, but for every class meeting.

Here we see the greatest contrast between systems where performance is measured once a year by an external examination, and the system in the United States, where faculty members begin measuring your performance almost immediately. On the second day of class, a judgment might be made about your mastery of a reading assignment, and on the third you may have to turn in homework to be graded. The first exam will likely take place within a month of term opening, and your mark on it will certainly influence your final grade.

You might think these ''sudden requirements'' have no purpose except to make you miserable. This is not so; to American educators, they have two solid justifications. First, of course, they enable the instructor to measure your abilities and performance. Just as importantly, they help *you* understand your abilities and performance. If you seem to be doing poorly in your physics course, you can drop it before a grade is assigned. If you have planned to major in engineering, you have now received a suggestion to consider majoring in another field, where a knowledge of physics is less important. If you have planned a major in physics, your instructor—or rather, your performance, as shown by your grade—is suggesting that you reanalyze your goals.

Moreover, you and your instructor now have a basis on which to discuss your abilities. Perhaps you can be a good physics student if you can figure out the instructor's (or the textbook's) way of presenting information. Visit the instructor during his or her office hours and talk about the matter.

MULTIPLE MEASUREMENTS

Examinations and other measurements of your knowledge and abilities not only occur suddenly, but they come in a series and they will probably be varied in nature. In the American view, several examinations are better than one, because on any single day a student may be distracted (for example, by illness) and perform poorly. The format of examinations will usually show variety as well: A set of

Figure 10-2 Cloze (Fill-in-the-Blank) Reading Test

2. The following is a paraphrase, or restatement, of the ideas in the reading passage. Key words have been omitted. Fill in the blank spaces *without reviewing the passage above.*

The author writes of the _____ provinces in _____ .
The major crop is _____ , but yields are often low due to
too little _____ . This area cannot grow _____ wheat,
and only in the _____ parts of the provinces is there a
reasonable yield of _____ wheat—and then, only when the
previous _____ is wet.

Annual yields therefore _____ widely. The 1962 crop was
almost _____ as large as the _____ crop. Another
good year was _____ . In brief, _____ latitudes do not
produce predictable crops.

The weather is particularly _____ at harvesting
season—for example, the month of _____ . In 1965, a delay
in harvesting caused by _____ reduced the value of the
wheat crop by $ _____ million. The fact that it was a
_____ crop meant not only that it contained less
_____ , but that _____ and facilities were inadequate.

SOURCE: G. Barnes, *Communication Skills for the Foreign-Born Professional* (Philadelphia: ISI Press, 1982), p. 122.

multiple-choice questions, a "fill-in-the-blank" section (see figure 10-2), and an essay may all appear on the same examination, or at least, on different examinations in the same course. Students who have difficulty writing but who know the material can prove their mastery on the objective, short-answer parts; students who have trouble with details but understand basic concepts can prove themselves in the essay. Instructors in mathematics will substitute problem-solving for the essay and instructors in other courses might set examinations containing short-answer or "matching-items" questions (see figure 10-3).

Moreover, examinations will not be the only measurement. Teachers understand that some students suffer from "test anxiety" and that they can better demonstrate their learning in other

Figure 10-3   Sample Matching-Items Test

ACTIVITY 18

The italicized word in each sentence below is a word you have already studied, though perhaps without the prefix. Match each with the correct definition.

1. The shows you want to watch are *nonconcurrent*.
2. It was an *unwieldy* burden.
3. Jeremy is a *nongregarious* young man.
4. Kathleen showed *unprecedented* generosity.
5. This tests your *nonverbal* skills.
6. We came through the storm *unscathed*.
7. She is in *unremitting* pain.
8. All these accounts are *nondelinquent*.
9. Stella is a very *undiscerning* young woman.
10. The moon is actually a *nonluminous* body.

a. not overdue

b. not seen before

c. not keen in judgment

d. not on at the same time

e. not involving words

f. not giving off light

g. not easy to handle

h. not harmed

i. not letting up

j. not sociable

SOURCE: Christine Beckert, *Vocabulary by Doing* (Lincolnwood, IL: National Textbook Company, 1990), p. 272.

ways. Thus, in the science courses, instructors may require lab reports and demonstrations in addition to examinations; mathematics instructors may mark homework assignments and weigh these marks heavily in assigning the final grade; a history course may require a paper, an engineering course a design project, a literature course an oral report.

And usually, in introductory courses particularly, there is the matter of participation, which may count for as much as 20 percent of your final grade. Of course, the instructor's evaluation of your interest and participation in a course is subjective, but it is considered a valid measure of your performance. It is simply another opportunity for you to demonstrate your learning and your special abilities.

INDIVIDUAL EFFORT IN ACADEMIC WORK

In this discussion of multiple measurements, you may have noticed the emphasis on individual effort and performance. Individualism is clearly a constant theme in American educational philosophy. It is important for you to understand this if you come from a culture where group effort and cooperation are valued over individual performance and competition. In the United States, your work on a class assignment must always be your own. Studying with a group is acceptable; completing your homework with the group's help is not.

Your friends cannot provide you answers for an examination or write a paper for you. Furthermore, in exams and papers, you cannot simply repeat words you have memorized from a book. Letting others provide you the answers in course assignments is considered academic dishonesty, and severe punishments are imposed.

For further understanding of this serious topic, see "Plagiarism" in chapter 11.

THE GRADING SYSTEM

Like everything else, grades arrive with alarming suddenness, and you may be shocked to discover that the instructor considers you an average or poor student, or that 70 percent correct on an examination does not earn you a high grade. Perhaps you already have a good knowledge of the standard grading system in the United States, but take a moment to review table 10-1, where a rough equivalency of grade, subjective meaning, and percentage of correct answers is shown. Much variation exists; the table indicates only associations most faculty and students make with the A-B-C-D-F scheme. In practice, an instructor will often give A's to the top 2 or 3 performers on an examination even if their answers are only 70 percent correct. The instructor's assumption here is that the examination, rather than the students' performance, was poor.

Your final grade for each course will be compiled from your grades in the various measurements. Out of the grades in all your courses, your term "grade-point average" will be calculated. Typi-

Table 10-1
A View of the American Grading System

Grade	Meaning in Words	Meaning in % Correct
A	Excellent	c. 91% +
B	Good	c. 82% to 90%
C	Fair; Average	c. 75% to 81%
D	Poor	c. 69% to 74%
F	Failing	c. 68%–

cally, an A is worth 4 points, a B, 3 points, and so on, for each credit in the course; thus, if you earned an A in a three-credit course, you would receive 12 grade points for it. To see how the process works, consider table 10-2. Your grade report shows that you took 15 credits and earned 48 grade points. By dividing 48 by 15, we determine that you have a 2.87 g.p.a. for the term.

Table 10-2
Sample Grade-Point Calculation

Course	Grade	Value	Credits	Grade-Points
Chemistry	A	4	3	12
Calculus	C	2	4	8
English	B	3	3	9
Chemistry Lab	D	1	2	2
History	A	4	3	12
			—	—
Term grade-point average: $43 \div 15 = 2.87$			15	43

After your second term of study, you will have a "cumulative grade-point average"—or as students commonly call it, a "cum" (kyume). That is, all your grade-points earned in the two terms, divided by all of the credits you have enrolled in at the school, yields your overall g.p.a. Your goal, of course, should be "straight As," or a "cum" of 4.0.

THE IMPORTANCE OF GRADES

Good grades are important, and it is very important *not* to receive F's. The system provides you a chance to avoid failing, because you will be allowed several weeks in which to drop a course in which you are performing badly. U.S. faculty members understand that there are many valid reasons for poor achievement in a course. Whereas they will fail you for academic dishonesty, they impose no penalty for withdrawing from a course before the deadline.

A second reason to avoid F's is that the Immigration and Naturalization Service expects you to successfully complete at least 12 credits (usually, four courses) each term. To be sure, dropping a course so that you are carrying fewer than 12 credits is also a problem; the INS will still say you have taken less than a full load. But generally, it is better to drop than to fail. The solution lies in planning wisely: Schedule yourself so that you do not risk failing.

Finally, F's are disastrous for your g.p.a., because they carry no grade points; the number of credits is simply added in. Meanwhile, the college or university will usually expect you to attain a cumulative grade-point average of 2.0—an overall C average—in order to continue in school. If you achieved below a 2.0 average for the term, or had less than a 2.0 cumulative average after the second term, you might be placed on probation. If your average continued to decline—so that your cumulative g.p.a. reached 1.5 or 1.3—you would be dropped from the university, and thus the INS would rule you "out of status." In case you find yourself in this sort of academic difficulty, you will need to seek the advice of the foreign student advisor, as well as that of your academic advisor.

But you are unlikely to be placed on probation, for two reasons:

- You already understand the need to begin working hard immediately.
- You will surely not enroll in a heavy load of courses (not more than five courses or 15 credits).

With a good start, in a reasonable courseload, you are more likely to receive grade reports showing A's and B's. Then you may find that you begin earning honors. You may make the "dean's list" of high-achieving students (typically, those who compile a 3.5 g.p.a.). Perhaps your name will be mentioned at an awards ceremony. Perhaps you will eventually *receive* an award. Meanwhile, in the registrar's office, a transcript of your work will be compiled, so that you will be able to demonstrate your success to your family and to prospective employers.

THE USE OF COMPUTERS

One of the newest features of American higher education remains to be mentioned: the use of computers, or computer-aided instruction. Computers are very much a part of college and university life, and not simply in administrative offices; faculty and students use them frequently in coursework. At one time, it was thought—or feared—that computers would "take over" the educational system and actually do much of the teaching. The takeover is not likely to happen very soon in the United States, perhaps because computers show little ability at interactive instruction.

Students preparing for professional life must know how to use computers as tools, however, and most educational institutions will encourage or even require computer work in completing course assignments; computer word-processing, for example, has replaced the typewriter as the standard technology for preparing papers in writing classes and graduate courses. Many colleges and universities provide huge banks of computer workstations (sometimes called "clusters") that remain open from early morning to late at night. A few institutions will actually require students to own per-

Figure 10-4   A University Computer "Cluster"

sonal computers; if you apply to one of these institutions, you must add the cost of a "P.C." to your budget.

You may be able to complete your college work without the use of a computer, but it will not be easy. Certainly you would be wise to learn how to type before you come to the United States, because computers have keyboards that are modeled on the typewriter's. Skill in typing will save you many hours of work in preparing your assignments.

A Three-Step Strategy for Success

From this chapter and chapter 9, we can set up three steps that will give you a good start toward successful undergraduate study. First, arrive early, rest, become familiar with your surroundings, and get your basic living needs under control. Second, seek the appropriate advice on scheduling, then choose courses carefully, and in your first term, enroll in a comparatively light load. Finally, keep up with each course's assignments from the very first day, and let your instructors see your *genuine* enthusiasm for their courses by participating in class interaction. Do not *pretend* to be enthusiastic, just to impress them; show a real interest.

Naturally, you must undergo an adjustment process just like anyone else in a strange country, and culture shock may slow your progress as a student. But whatever else happens, meet your instructors' deadlines, show interest in your classes, and you will find yourself becoming increasingly successful as a student.

CHAPTER 11

ADJUSTING TO GRADUATE STUDIES

THIS CONCLUDING CHAPTER ADDRESSES THOSE PERSONS WHO ARE ABOUT to become international graduate students in American universities. If you are a prospective graduate student or applicant, you probably passed over chapter 10, in which case you will have missed useful information, because some of the characteristics of the undergraduate classroom—interactiveness, say, or multiple measurements—are also true of the graduate classroom. And indeed, there is a graduate classroom, as we will discuss.

First it should be said that your acceptance into a graduate program in the United States will mean that you have been elected into the body of scholars, for you have competed against many other students to earn this status. It will mean also that you have successfully taken very difficult exams—the GRE, GMAT, or an equivalent—and achieved a TOEFL score that suggests near-native fluency in English. Assuming that, in fact, you have now been accepted for graduate study, it means that you are about to enter a realm, in American education, where the "B student" is only an average student. Thus, you will need to come to your new work prepared to demonstrate excellence.

"Graduate study" means more, in the United States, than just study toward a master's or Ph.D.: There are post-baccalaureate professional schools (usually attached to universities) of education, law, medicine, and various medical subfields leading to the Ed.D., J.D., M.D., and so on. But education for the professions is not directly considered in this chapter. If you are seeking to begin study in medicine or law, write for information directly to the Association of American Medical Colleges or the Association of American Law Schools, both at the same address:

**One Dupont Circle
Washington, DC 20036 USA**

The requirements outlined below apply generally to almost all other graduate and professional programs.

RESEARCH AND THE AMERICAN UNIVERSITY

We will begin by reviewing the special atmosphere of a good university in the United States. You should understand, above all, that you are entering a research-oriented environment. In some countries, high-level research is mainly undertaken outside of educational institutions. In the United States, universities are responsible for a large proportion of the nation's research effort; they account for about US$12 *billion* a year in research and development. From your earliest days at the university, you may be urged to carry out research that will prove either publishable or fundable. Many professors in the sciences and engineering spend more time writing grants and carrying out funded research than they do teaching.

The availability of research funding is extremely attractive in the United States, particularly as compared to the situation in most other countries; research grants may come from the federal or state governments, from rich philanthropic foundations, from professional organizations, or from industry. The competition to gain such funds is fierce, however. As a result, grant application forms demand greater and greater detail, as funding agencies seek to make distinctions between hundreds of applicants. If you are a graduate student in the sciences or the engineering fields, you may discover that your professor needs a grant to provide you a research assistantship—if not this term, then next term.

University administrations are enthusiastic about grants, for several reasons. First, a grant traditionally includes "overhead"—a percentage of the researcher's request that will go to the university for administrative support (including the new equipment and facilities that will keep the institution up to date). The grant will usually include money to provide the researcher time off from teaching; the university can replace him or her with a junior instructor at a lower salary. The researcher's own funds will often provide money for research assistants—for you, if you are fortunate—and the university can therefore attract high-quality graduate students by offering them financial support. Grants also bring good publicity, even newspaper articles. And they tend to bring more grants: A grant to study solar energy makes the university seem a leader in solar energy research, and thus, from the viewpoint of other grant-making agencies, a good institution to sponsor for further research in that field.

As a new graduate student, you cannot expect to write successful grant applications or even to suggest good fundable ideas. As time goes on, however, you may participate in a team that carries out funded research and then in a team that puts together a grant proposal. The ability to work well with a team is a particularly important skill in the science and technical fields.

The situation is much different in the liberal arts and social sciences. Research is more often an individual effort, with the faculty's guidance; funding—or at least, large funding—is much less likely. Here the goal is publication, and although relatively few graduate students publish, they are encouraged to work toward that goal. Research is, without doubt, the most widely respected activity throughout the American university.

THE UNIVERSITY LIBRARY

A university can be a great research institution only if it has the facilities that make high-level research possible. It is well-known that the leading American universities have modern and extensive laboratories, but perhaps less well-known that some of the nation's most comprehensive libraries are found on their campuses. The library at the University of California/Berkeley, for example, contains about 104,000 "current serials"—that is, current issues of periodical publications such as magazines and journals. The Harvard library contains nearly 12 million volumes and employs more than 1000 staff members. At least one hundred other university li-

Figure 11-1   Study Space in a University Library

braries count their collections in the millions of volumes; almost literally, they seek to own every book, journal, and document that may be of use to any of their faculty members. If you have chosen a university that is strong in your major discipline, its library is likely to have a very deep collection in that discipline, because the faculty will insist on it.

You should plan to visit your university's library soon after your arrival. You will find it much more than a repository of books and journals, even though the collection is its most important feature. Reference librarians will be available to help you locate obscure publications. Computer databases will be available, at little or no charge, to help you retrieve information. An inter-library loan office will be available to help you borrow books from other libraries.

Aiding the institution's research mission is the library's first priority. You will find plenty of quiet, well-lighted work space: tables, comfortable chairs, private rooms, and carrels (small workstations); the accompanying picture shows a typical public space in a university library. Probably you will be able to roam freely through the stacks, searching for the publications you want. The library provides so much encouragement for scholarly work that you may choose to spend your evenings there, even if you are simply studying from your textbooks.

COURSEWORK

Your first surprise, in preparing for graduate study or actually beginning your studies, will be to learn that there are courses to complete. In many other countries' university systems, the doctoral degree requires only the completion of a research project under the close supervision of a faculty member. In these or other systems the master's degree may be little more than an honorary award. Neither of these situations is true of graduate degrees in the United States. There are a number of steps to complete in graduate studies, the first of which is a set of required courses.

Why this should be true is not important; the reason probably lies in slow specialization, although coursework also allows other professors—in addition to your major advisor—to measure your ability and to provide you challenges and insights. The fact is that, like undergraduates, you will buy textbooks, take examinations, and meet requirements stated on course outlines, probably for at least one and one-half years. In some cases you may occasionally find undergraduates in the same courses with you. Unlike them, you will be required to write a paper or to carry out a "graduate-level" project in order to earn graduate credit in the course.

Like an undergraduate, you too will compile a grade-point average (see chapter 10), and your grades can have a considerable impact on your future opportunities. Usually, a "three-point oh" (3.0) g.p.a.—that is, a B average—is necessary to avoid probation; if you receive a C, which means "average" in undergraduate work, you have essentially failed a graduate course. Two or three consecutive terms in which you have received C's, or built a cumulative average below 3.0, would probably mean that you would be dropped from the university. Neither probation nor dismissal is likely to happen to you, but until you have adjusted to the system, you may struggle to achieve the grades you should achieve.

THE PROFESSOR AS MENTOR

In chapter 10, we reviewed the interactive classroom—the constant questioning, discussion, and meetings between faculty members and students—common to undergraduate study in the United States. The same general situation will hold in your graduate classes. The faculty will take an interest in you and your work and make themselves available to speak with you. Some of your courses will be seminars, which are very small classes in which discussion among professor and students goes on continuously.

With undergraduates, the faculty play almost a parental role. Toward you as a graduate student, however, they serve more as guides or mentors. The difference is that they are not so much measuring your intellectual ability as directing you toward scholarly production. They assume that you are intelligent; only students with scholarly ability or potential are admitted to graduate school. They expect you to work independently after they have given you a start. The good news in this is that you are being treated almost as an equal; the hard part is that your professors will challenge you and criticize your work.

The ability to accept criticism is a necessary skill of the graduate student. Faculty members will not publicly disparage your performance, but they are likely to challenge your work repeatedly. At first, you may feel like you are being shamed—that you are losing face. If you are wise, however, you will see that fair, objective criticism is necessary to learning, and certainly necessary for anyone who wishes to be a successful graduate student. Whenever professors question your data or your findings, assume you must go back to work and answer their criticisms positively.

THE GRADUATE STUDENT WORKLOAD

Graduate students are often the most overworked people on a university campus—or anywhere else. This is particularly true if they have teaching assistantships. The teaching assistant is simultaneously teacher, student, and researcher (because, presumably, he or she is preparing to do, or actually doing, original research leading to a degree). The teaching assignment may be only six hours per week, but for inexperienced instructors, six hours of teaching can mean forty or more hours of preparation, administration, and follow-up. The assignments given by professors in graduate courses are also heavy.

As an international graduate student, you are likely to face additional problems. Culture shock is the best known of these; fortunately, its effects are temporary but they can prevent you from working efficiently. By definition, you are also an outsider, even if you are well adjusted. Your family is far away; the foods you like are hard to get; you have more difficulty using telephones, public transportation, the postal system, and so on. In the beginning of your studies, at least, you need extra time to master local life. Thus, you should not start off too ambitiously—for example, by enrolling in a heavy courseload. The Immigration and Naturalization Service requires you to take nine credits (usually, three courses), and you would be wise to take precisely nine credits. If you need help with your English, ask the foreign student advisor's permission to enroll in five or six credits plus an English course.

The other hardship in the international student workload is indeed the language barrier. In a recent study, ten international teaching assistants with limited English proficiency were asked to divide their work into weekly hours: time spent in class, time spent teaching, time spent on personal matters. The greatest amount of time was needed to do the reading for their own graduate courses—*more than forty hours each week*. Studying was, in short, a full-time job. Going to class, preparing to teach, and teaching itself were simply additional tasks.

MAINTAINING YOUR HEALTH AND SAFETY

Several facts of graduate student life raise questions about your health and well-being, particularly if you are supported by an assistantship. Your workload is obviously one of them; you may find it embarrassing to inform your advisor that you cannot maintain the workload that has been asked of you, but you must do so if you feel you have insufficient time for rest and recreation. Similarly, you must find ways to eat nutritious food despite your small income.

A few words need to be said, as well, about laboratory safety. Both research and teaching assistants, in the science and engineering fields, will encounter hazardous situations and materials in university laboratories. Accidents have cost universities millions of dollars and put students' health at risk. Within a few days in 1990, for example, a professor and four workers were exposed to radiation in the biomedical lab of one university, and eight students were exposed to infected animals at the veterinary farm of another.

Given these dangers, you need to take precautions. You have a right to information about laboratory hazards and a right to receive safety training. Too often, training is omitted by departments because there is no time for it—or because graduate assistants themselves are overconfident. Again, you may be embarrassed to ask your department for training, but it is appropriate and necessary for you to ask: You are in a new country dealing with expensive equipment or volatile chemicals, and however intelligent and well-trained you are, you can take on laboratory responsibilities only if you are well informed.

Figure 11-2   Graduate Students in a University Laboratory *(Photo courtesy of the Public Information Office, Drexel University)*

Your need is particularly great if you have difficulty communicating in English. As has been suggested several times in this book, English needs to come first in your educational plan. If the admissions office tells you that you must enroll in an English course before you can be fully admitted, do not resist that advice. The time you "lose" studying English is a small price for the mental and physical well-being that come from good communication skills; moreover, that time will be made up as you study, later, for the courses in your graduate program.

THE MASTER'S PROGRAM

A master's course in the United States is a program of one to two years' duration, consisting mostly of coursework. In fact, the "master's thesis" that used to be standard is no longer frequently required. Rather, a set of courses—perhaps ten of them, or roughly thirty semester credits—constitutes the main requirement. In some fields (for example, nutrition and psychology), clinical internships are a mandatory part of the program, reflecting the emphasis of American education on practical applications. Depending on the program, a master's examination (sometimes called "comps," for "comprehensive") may be required.

The master's degree may or may not be a step toward the Ph.D. In certain fields, the master's is the terminal (highest) degree; the best-known example is the "M.F.A.," or Master of Fine Arts. The Master's of Business Administration (MBA) used to be the terminal degree in business, and it is still a much more common objective than the Ph.D. An MBA graduate with plans for further education is as likely to go into law as into a doctoral course in business administration. Increasingly, graduate business programs are taking on international student enrollment, as the MBA grows in status among foreign companies and governments.

In certain cases, the master's degree is awarded when the student has finished the necessary work but shows little promise for doctoral studies; such a determination may be made on the basis of the comprehensive exams mentioned above. You would not choose to earn a master's under these circumstances, of course. But if you wish to work in industry, a master's degree—particularly an MBA or an M.S. in science or engineering—is virtually as good as a doctorate. A career in research or university teaching will more likely require the Ph.D.

The Doctoral Program

Doctoral studies usually require about five years of very hard work. The time may be shorter if you are allowed to bypass master's degree requirements; it may be longer if you take on a dissertation project that requires extensive research. Approximately half the program is needed to complete coursework; the other half—often the most painful—is usually consumed in dissertation research and writing. Along the way, there are at least three other requirements to meet:

- *A minor field.* Even at doctoral level, students may be required to complete coursework for a ''minor'' in fields related to, but apart from, their major fields. Given the strong interest in interdisciplinary studies today, that emphasis will continue: You will probably be required to show proficiency in a subject outside your major specialization.
- *Qualifying examinations.* Students will usually be admitted to doctoral candidacy only through the successful completion of an extensive examination. Occasionally this will be the ''comps,'' but it could be another set of tests, written or oral, called the ''qualifying'' or ''preliminary'' exams—known familiarly as ''orals,'' ''quals,'' or ''prelims.'' Often such examinations last an entire day or even several days, and require months of preparation.
- *Foreign language requirements.* Traditionally, the doctoral candidate is required to master two ''foreign'' languages (i.e., besides English). The level of mastery is not fluency, but many graduate students have found themselves working diligently at French or German or another language in which

scholarly literature is published. Some universities or departments will allow international students to substitute their mother tongues for one of these. Some will allow a university foreign language department to certify students' mastery of the relevant language, but others will require that they show proficiency via a standardized examination.

There is also an increasing tendency to demand evidence of "tool" mastery—the ability to use computers as research tools, to create computer programs, to make statistical analyses, and so on.

The Dissertation

The dissertation nevertheless remains the greatest assignment to complete on the road to the Ph.D. It requires considerable initiative. Major professors do not set dissertation topics for graduate students, because candidates for an advanced degree are expected to know what they want to study and how to set up a research project.

Then, at each step, the doctoral candidate encounters difficult decisions and pressures:

- An idea *that no one else has investigated* (or investigated in the same way) must be found.
- A faculty advisor or committee must be persuaded that the research is worth doing.
- The research itself will be lonely and probably frustrating, as your original hypothesis proves unworkable, or at least, in need of modification.
- The writing rarely goes as fast as you think it will.
- Your advisor may tell you that you are headed in the wrong direction and should start over.
- You will likely need to rewrite substantial portions of your work when you are already thinking of taking a job or returning home.
- You will be required to defend your dissertation to a faculty group that will criticize it.

Every survivor of a graduate program remembers these pressures.

At least 50 percent of doctoral candidates succeed in completing their degree programs, and you must prepare yourself psychologically to be among them. The best advice on getting ready for dissertation research is to begin looking for a topic and a dissertation advisor during the first, "easy" part of the program; before you finish your coursework, you should become a near-expert on that topic. Your dissertation will then seem a logical next step. Once you are fully engaged in your research, you might also ask your advisor to establish a timetable for bringing it to a close and then for the submission of each chapter. The timetable will be artificial, but it can stimulate you to get the writing done.

The other half of the students in your program will be less fortunate. Many doctoral candidates continue to enroll year after year, thinking that, finally, they will get their dissertations written. The university imposes a time limit, however, and at the end of that time—perhaps, seven years—informs these students that they will no longer be eligible to receive their Ph.D.'s. Other candidates give up before the limit is reached, knowing that they cannot write what is essentially a book; they refer to themselves as "ABD's," meaning "all but dissertation."

Plagiarism

Obviously, the competition is very strong in graduate and professional education. All your fellow students are intelligent, and sometimes they compete with you for research assistantships or postgraduate positions. The pressure is also strong on everyone to produce: papers for courses, dissertations, articles for publication, and so on. Some students will be tempted to take shortcuts—to borrow other people's ideas rather than to do the original research that is expected of graduate students. You may find the temptation especially strong if you lack the English skills to compete with native-speaking students in the writing of papers and other required documents. The consequences could be disastrous, and thus a moment must be spent here on this unpleasant topic.

A cultural division exists between "Western" cultures and some other cultures on the ownership of ideas and words. In other cultures, a student's use of scholars' ideas or repetition of their language may seem like compliments to those scholars. In the United States, by contrast, original ideas and language are considered scholars' *property.* Thus, plagiarism—the use of other people's ideas or words as though they were your own—is considered a serious offense; it is equated with theft.

At least once a year, headlines in major newspapers announce that a successful scholar has been forced to resign from a prestigious position because of published work that proves to be plagiarized rather than original. Sometimes these persons are not even aware of their ''theft'': An assistant has provided them with information or language that they then use in a publication. Still, they are the ones punished; it is always the scholar's responsibility to check sources and to give credit (''attribution'') in notes within their own texts.

Plagiarism can cause universities to deny degrees and to expel students. Obviously you must be very careful in your own work. Failure to provide attribution to others for their ideas is always a mistake. Even asking a typist to ''clean up'' your English is a questionable act. You would then submit a written product that belongs only partially to you.

RELATIONSHIPS WITH MEMBERS OF YOUR DEPARTMENT

One last suggestion should be made to you as a prospective graduate student at an American university: Be a strong member of your departmental team. This theme has already been seen in various other sections of the chapter. You have read about the importance of teamwork in scientific research; you have learned that you must accept criticism in order to do your best work; and you have surely accepted the need for scrupulous honesty in separating your ideas and words from those of other scholars.

But there are still other reasons for working closely with your professors and fellow students. You are all part of a comparatively small group of specialists, and you will need one another in years to come. Your colleagues are the people who can help you solve research problems, even if they are half the world away from you.

They are also people who can write letters of recommendation for you when you seek jobs or grants.

The faculty are especially important to your future, and your major professor is the most important person of all. Serve an apprenticeship to this person gladly and loyally. In return, he or she will help you find a meaningful dissertation project, support your candidacy for the doctorate, and perhaps nominate you for work with an exciting research team. Moreover, your professor may help you find a publisher for that first article that establishes you in your field—or let you co-author one of his or her own articles for which you have provided research assistance. Not all professors are so generous with their graduate students, but your loyal support will improve your chances of gaining their support in return.

Later, your major professor's letter of recommendation will be particularly meaningful as you take on new challenges in your career. By serving as a team player during your graduate studies, you create a desire in others to continue their association with you. The rewards will likely follow you throughout your professional life.

LIST OF EDUCATIONAL ADVISING CENTER LOCATIONS

Algeria	Algiers
Antigua & Barbuda	St. Johns
Argentina	Buenos Aires
Australia	Canberra
Austria	Vienna
Bahamas	Nassau
Bahrain	Manama
Bangladesh	Dhaka
Barbados	Bridgetown
Belgium	Brussels
Belize	Belize City
Benin	Cotonou
Bermuda	Devonshire
Bolivia	Cochabamba, La Paz, Santa Cruz
Botswana	Gaborone
Brazil	Belém, Belo Horizonte, Brasília, Curitiba, Florianópolis, Fortaleza, Manaus, Pôrto Alegre, Recife, Rio de Janeiro, Salvador, São Luís, São Paulo, Vitória
Brunei	Bandar Seri Begawan
Bulgaria	Sofia
Burkina Faso	Ouagadougou
Burma	Rangoon
Burundi	Bujumbura
Cameroon	Douala, Yaounde
Canada	Ottawa
Cape Verde	Praia
Central African Republic	Bangui
Chad	N'Djamena
Chile	Antofagasta, Concepción, Santiago, Valparaíso

China, People's Republic of	Beijing, Changchun, Chengdu, Chongqing, Dalian, Guangzhou, Harbin, Shanghai, Shenyang, Wuchang, Xi'an
Colombia	Armenia, Barranquilla, Bogotá, Bucaramanga, Cali, Cartagena, Manizales, Medellín, Pereira
Comoros	Moroni
Congo	Brazzaville
Costa Rica	San José
Cuba	Havana
Cyprus	Nicosia
Czechoslovakia	Prague
Denmark	Copenhagen
Djibouti	Djibouti
Dominican Republic	Santiago de los Caballeros, Santo Domingo
Ecuador	Guayaquil, Quito
Egypt	Alexandria, Cairo
El Salvador	San Salvador
England	London
Equatorial Guinea	Malabo
Ethiopia	Addis Ababa
Fiji	Suva
Finland	Helsinki
France	Bordeaux, Lyons, Marseilles, Paris, Strasbourg
French Caribbean Dep't.	Fort-de-France
Gabon	Libreville
The Gambia	Banjul
Germany	Berlin, Bonn, Cologne, Frankfurt, Hamburg, Hannover, Munich, Stuttgart
Ghana	Accra
Greece	Athens, Salonika
Grenada	St. George's
Guatemala	Guatemala City
Guinea	Conakry
Guyana	Georgetown
Haiti	Port-au-Prince
Honduras	San Pedro Sula, Tegucigalpa (Comayaguela)
Hong Kong	Wanchai
Hungary	Budapest
Iceland	Reykjavik
India	Bombay, Calcutta, Madras, New Delhi
Indonesia	Jakarta, Medan, Surabaya
Iraq	Baghdad
Ireland	Dublin
Israel	Jerusalem, Tel Aviv
Italy	Florence, Genoa, Milan, Naples, Palermo, Rome, Turin

Ivory Coast	Abidjan
Jamaica	Kingston
Japan	Tokyo
Jordan	Amman, Irbid
Kenya	Mombasa, Nairobi
Korea	Seoul
Kuwait	Kuwait
Lebanon	Antelias, Beirut
Lesotho	Maseru
Liberia	Monrovia
Luxembourg	Luxembourg
Madagascar	Antananarivo
Malawi	Lilongwe
Malaysia	Kuala Lumpur, Penang
Mali	Bamako
Malta	Floriana
Mauritania	Nouakchott
Mauritius	Port Louis
Mexico	Chihuahua, Guadalajara, Hermosillo, Mérida, Mexico City, Monterrey, Morelia, Saltillo, San Luis Potosí, Tampico, Torreón, Veracruz, Zacatecas
Morocco	Casablanca, Fès, Kenitra, Marrakech, Rabat, Tangier, Tétouan
Nepal	Katmandu
Netherlands	Amsterdam
New Zealand	Wellington
Nicaragua	Managua
Niger	Niamey
Nigeria	Ibadan, Kaduna, Lagos
Northern Ireland	Belfast
Norway	Oslo, Tromsö
Oman	Muscat
Pakistan	Islamabad, Karachi, Lahore, Peshawar
Panama	Panama City
Papua New Guinea	Port Moresby
Paraguay	Asunción
Peru	Arequipa, Chiclayo, Cuzco, Lima, Trujillo
Philippines	Cebu City, Davao City, Manila
Poland	Kraków, Poznań, Warsaw
Portugal	Lisbon
Qatar	Doha
Romania	Bucharest
Rwanda	Kigali
Saudi Arabia	Dhahran, Jidda, Riyadh
Senegal	Dakar
Seychelles	Victoria
Sierra Leone	Freetown

Singapore	Singapore
South Africa	Cape Town, Durban, Johannesburg, Pretoria
Spain	Barcelona, Madrid
Sri Lanka	Colombo
Sudan	Khartoum
Surinam	Paramaribo
Swaziland	Mbabane
Sweden	Stockholm
Switzerland	Bern, Zurich
Syria	Damascus
Taiwan	Taipei
Tanzania	Dar es Salaam
Thailand	Bangkok, Chiangmai, Songkhla
Togo	Lome
Trinidad and Tobago	Port of Spain
Tunisia	Tunis
Turkey	Ankara, Istanbul
Uganda	Kampala
U.S.S.R.	Leningrad, Moscow
United Arab Emirates	Abu Dhabi, Dubai
United Kingdom	See England and Northern Ireland
Uruguay	Montevideo
Venezuela	Caracas, Maracaibo
Yemen Arab Republic	Sana'a
Yugoslavia	Belgrade, Ljubljana, Sarajevo, Skopje, Titograd, Zagreb
Zaire	Kinshasa
Zambia	Lusaka
Zimbabwe	Harare

SOURCE: College Entrance Examination Board, *1989-90 Directory of Overseas Educational Advising Centers* (New York: CEEB, 1989).

APPENDIX 2

MINIMUM REFERENCE BOOKSHELF
FOR EDUCATIONAL ADVISING CENTERS

AACJC (American Association of Community and Junior Colleges) Guide to Community, Technical and Junior Colleges
Accredited Institutions of Post-Secondary Education
Accredited Programs Leading to Degrees in Engineering
Accredited Programs Leading to Degrees in Engineering Technology
Adviser's Manual of Federal Regulations Affecting Foreign Students and Scholars
Advising Quarterly
Allied Health Education Directory
Arrival Information Requests
The College Handbook: Index of Majors, Foreign Student Supplement
A Comparative Guide to American Colleges
Directory of Graduate Medical Education Programs
Directory of Graduate Programs
Directory of Home Study Schools
Directory of Overseas Educational Advising Centers
Diversity, Accessibility, and Quality: A Brief Introduction to American Education for Non-Americans
The Doctor of Philosophy Degree
Engineering College Research and Graduate Study
English Language and Orientation Programs in the United States
Foreign Teaching Assistants in U.S. Universities
Funding for U.S. Study: A Guide for Foreign Nationals
Handbook of Private Accredited Trade and Technical Schools
Higher Education Directory
If You Want to Study in the U.S.
Lovejoy's College Guide
NAFSA (National Association for Foreign Student Affairs) Directory
NAFSA Newsletter
Occupational Outlook Handbook
Official Guide to MBA Programs, Admissions and Careers
Open Doors: Report on International Educational Exchange
Overseas Educational Advisers' Manual
Peterson's Annual Guides to Graduate Study
Peterson's Annual Guides to Undergraduate Study
Profiles: The Foreign Student in the United States
Request for Application Materials from U.S. Colleges and Universities
Specialized Study Options

SOURCE: United States Information Agency, *Bibliography for Educational Advising Centers* (Washington: Unpublished document, 1989).

LIST OF INTERNATIONAL TOEFL AND TSE TEST CENTER LOCATIONS
(TSE TEST CENTERS INDICATED BY AN ASTERISK[*])

Algeria	Alger
Argentina	Buenos Aires*, Cordoba, Mendoza, Rosario, Tucuman
Australia	Adelaide, Brisbane, Canberra, Melbourne*, Perth, Sydney*
Austria	Graz*, Innsbruck*, Vienna*
Bahamas	Freeport
Bahrain	Juffair
Bangladesh	Dhaka*
Belgium	Antwerp*, Brussels*, Waterloo
Belize	Belize City
Benin	Cotonou
Bermuda	Paget
Bolivia	Cochabamba, La Paz*, Santa Cruz
Botswana	Gaborone*
Brazil	Belém, Belo Horizonte*, Brasília, Campinas, Curitiba, Fortaleza, Londrina, Pôrto Alegre*, Recife*, Rio de Janeiro*, Salvador, São Paulo*, Vicosa
Brunei	Bandar Seri Begawan
Bulgaria	Sofia*
Burkina Faso	Ouagadougou
Burma	Rangoon
Burundi	Bujumbura
Cameroon	Douala*, Yaounde
Central African Republic	Bangui
Chile	Antofagasta, Concepción, Santiago*

China, People's Republic of	Beijing*, Changsha*, Chengdu*, Chongqing*, Dalian*, Guangzhou*, Hangzhou*, Harbin*, Hefei*, Jinan*, Kunming*, Lanzhou*, Luo Yang*, Nanchang*, Nanjing*, Qingdao*, Shanghai*, Shenzhen*, Shijiazhuang*, Taiyuan*, Tianjin*, Urumgi, Wuhan*, Xiamen*, Xi'an*
Colombia	Barranquilla, Bogotá*, Bucaramanga, Cali, Cartagena, Medellín*
Congo	Brazzaville
Costa Rica	San José*
Cyprus	Limassol*, Nicosia*
Czechoslovakia	Prague
Denmark	Copenhagen*, Odense
Djibouti	Djibouti
Dominican Republic	Santiago, Santo Domingo
Ecuador	Guayaquil, Quito*
Egypt	Alexandria*, Cairo*
El Salvador	San Salvador
England	Birmingham, Hunmanby/Filey, London*, Manchester*, Marshfield, Newcastle Upon Tyne, Thorpe (Surrey), Uxbridge
Ethiopia	Addis Ababa*, Asmara
Fiji	Suva*
Finland	Helsinki*
France	Aix-en-Provence*, Angers*, Besançon, Bordeaux, Brest, Caen, Grenoble, Le Havre, Lille*, Lyons*, Lyon/Villeurbane, Marseilles*, Montpellier*, Nancy, Nice*, Noisy-le-Grand*, Paris*, Pau, Poitiers, Strasbourg, Toulouse*, Valbonne*
Gabon	Libreville
Gambia	Banjul
Gaza Strip	Gaza
Germany	Aachen*, Berlin, Bonn*, Cologne, Düsseldorf*, Frankfurt*, Freiburg*, Göttingen, Hamburg*, Hannover, Kassel*, Ludwigsburg, Munich, Munich/Starnberg, Oberursel, Stuttgart*, Tübingen

Ghana	Accra*
Greece	Athens*, Patras, Salonika*
Guatemala	Guatemala City*, Quezaltenango
Guinea	Conakry*
Guyana	Georgetown*
Haiti	Les Cayes, Port-au-Prince*
Honduras	La Ceiba, San Pedro Sula, Tegucigalpa*
Hong Kong	Hong Kong*
Hungary	Budapest
Iceland	Reykjavik*
India	Ahmedabad*, Allahabad*, Bangalore*, Bhopal, Bhubaneswar, Bombay*, Calcutta*, Chochin (Thevara), Coimbatore, Delhi*, Gauhati, Hyderabad, Kanpur, Lucknow, Madras*, Madurai, Nagpur, New Delhi*, Pune, Secunderabad, Thimphu (Bhutan), Trivandrum*
Indonesia	Ambon, Banda Aceh, Bandung, Banjarmasin, Bengkulu, Bogor, Denpasar, Duri, Jakarta*, Jayapura, Kendari, Malang, Manado, Medan*, Padang, Palembang, Pekanbaru, Surabaya*, Udjung Pandang*, Yogyakarta*
Iraq	Baghdad*
Ireland	Dublin*
Israel	Haifa, Jerusalem*, Tel Aviv*
Italy	Bari*, Florence*, Genoa*, Milan*, Naples, Padua, Rome, Turin, Trieste
Ivory Coast	Abidjan
Jamaica	Kingston
Japan	Aichi*, Chiba, Fukuoka, Fukushima, Gumma, Himeji, Hiratsuka, Hiroshima*, Ibaraki, Kawasaki, Kitakyushu, Kobe*, Kyoto, Miyazaki, Nagasaki, Naha*, Niigata, Oita, Okayama, Osaka, Saitama, Sapporo*, Sendai, Shimonoseki, Shizuoka, Tokyo*, Toyama, Yokohama
Jordan	Amman*, Irbid

Kenya	Mombasa, Nairobi*
Korea	Buchon, Chonju, Chunchon, Kwangju, Pusan, Seoul*, Taegu, Taejon
Kuwait	Khaldiya, Shweikh*
Lebanon	Beirut*
Lesotho	Roma
Liberia	Monrovia
Luxembourg	Luxembourg
Macao	Macao
Madagascar	Antananarivo
Malawi	Zomba*
Malaysia	Alor Setar (Kedah), Ipoh (Perak), Johore Bahru, Kota Bharu (Kelantan), Kuala Lumpur*, Kuala Terengganu, Kuantan (Pahag), Malacca, Penang, Sabah*, Sarawak, Seremban (Negri Sembilan)
Mali	Bamako
Malta	Msida*
Martinique	Fort-de-France
Mauritius	Reduit*
Mexico	Chiapas, Chihuahua, Guadalajara*, Hermosillo, La Paz, Mérida, Mexico City*, Monterrey, Puebla, Veracruz
Morocco	Casablanca, Marrakesh, Rabat*, Tangier
Mozambique	Maputo
Namibia	Ondangwa, Windhoek
Nepal	Katmandu
Netherlands	Amsterdam, Arnhem*, The Hague
Netherlands Antilles	Aruba, Bonaire Island, Curaçao, St. Maarten
New Caldonia	Chamber of Commerce
New Zealand	Auckland*, Wellington
Nicaragua	Managua
Niger	Niamey
Nigeria	Abeokuta, Benin City, Calabar, Enugu*, Ibadan, Jos, Kaduna*, Kano*, Lagos, Owerri, Port Harcourt
Norway	Bergen*, Hafrsfjord*, Kristiansand, Oslo*, Tromsö, Trondheim*
Oman	Muscat

Pakistan	Hyderabad, Islamabad, Karachi, Lahore*, Peshawar*
Panama	Balboa*, Panama City
Papua New Guinea	Lae, Port Moresby
Paraguay	Asunción
Peru	Arequipa, Ilo, La Oroya, Lima*
Philippines	Baguio, Cagayan de Oro, Cebu City*, Davao City*, Dumaguete, Iloilo, Los Baños*, Makati, Quezon City*, San Fernando
Poland	Warsaw*
Portugal	Lisbon*, Oporto
Qatar	Doha*
Romania	Bucharest
Rwanda	Kigali
Saint Lucia	Castries
Saudi Arabia	Dammam, Dhahran, Jidda*, Riyadh*
Scotland	Glasgow*
Senegal	Dakar
Seychelles	Victoria*
Sierra Leone	Freetown*
Singapore	Singapore*
Somalia	Mogadishu
South Africa	Alice, Bellville, Cape Town, Durban*, Durban-Westville, Esikhawini, Johannesburg*, Mmabatho, Phuthaditjhaba, Pietersburg, Port Elizabeth, Rocklands, Sovenga, Soweto, Umtata
Spain	Barcelona*, Bilbao*, Las Palmas, Lugo*, Madrid*, Mallorca, Seville, Valencia
Sri Lanka	Colombo*
Sudan	Khartoum*
Suriname	Paramaribo
Swaziland	Mbabane*
Sweden	Goteborg*, Lulea*, Lund*, Stockholm*
Switzerland	Bern*, Chesieres-Villars, Geneva*, Kilchberg (Zurich)*, Leysin, Lugano, Montreux, St. Gallen*
Syria	Aleppo, Damascus*

Tahiti	Papeete
Taiwan	Taipei*
Tanzania	Dar es Salaam*, Moshi
Thailand	Bangkok*, Chiang Mai*, Khon Kaen, Songkhla
Togo	Lome*
Tonga	Neiafu/Vava'u, Nuku'alofa/Tongatapu
Trinidad and Tobago	Port of Spain
Tunisia	Tunis*
Turkey	Ankara*, Istanbul*, Izmir, Tarsus
Uganda	Kampala
U.S.S.R.	Moscow
United Arab Emirates	Abu Dhabi, Al-Ain, Dubai, Sharjah
United Kingdom	See England, Scotland, and Wales
Uruguay	Montevideo*
Venezuela	Caracas*, Maracaibo*, Puerto Ordaz, Valencia
Wales	Swansea
West Bank	Birzeit, Hebron, Jerusalem
Yemen Arab Republic	Sana'a*, Taiz
Yugoslavia	Belgrade*, Zagreb
Zaire	Kinshasa*, Lubumbashi
Zambia	Lusaka*
Zimbabwe	Bulawayo, Harare*

SOURCE: Educational Testing Service, *TOEFL and TSE 1990–91 Test Center Reference List, Revised Edition* (Princeton: ETS, 1990).

SAMPLE UNDERGRADUATE APPLICATION FOR ADMISSION

Drexel University
PHILADELPHIA PENNSYLVANIA

FRESHMAN AND TRANSFER STUDENT APPLICATION FOR ADMISSION TO FULL-TIME PROGRAMS

DESIRED STATUS (Please read the explanation of each status in the instructions before checking one.)

Freshman Admissions (check one)
☐ Early Decision Freshman for September 1991 *(Deadline November 15)*.
☐ Regular Decision Freshman for September 1991 *(Deadline March 1)*.
☐ Early Admission Freshman for September 1991 *(Deadline March 1)*.

Transfer Admissions (check one)
☐ Transfer Student for September 1991 *(Deadline August 15)*.
☐ Transfer Student for January 1992 *(Deadline November 15)*.
☐ Transfer Student for March 1992 *(Deadline February 15)*.
☐ Transfer Student for June 1992 *(Deadline May 15)*.

Please type or print clearly. Attach to this form your check or money order for the non-refundable $25 application fee. Make check payable to Drexel University.

1. _____   Your Social Security number will become your Admissions ID number and should clearly be
   Social Security Number   shown on all correspondence. (Non-citizens will be assigned an ID number.)

2. Applicant's Full Name _____
   Last (family)   First   Middle   Suffix

3. Permanent
   Address _____ _____
           No. & Street   Apartment No.

   _____ _____
   Town or City   State   Zip Code

   _____
   Country

4. Temporary   Between dates of _____ and _____
   Address

   _____ _____
   No. & Street   Apartment No.

   _____ _____
   Town or City   State   Zip Code

Telephone (_____)
Area Code

Country

Telephone (_____)
Area Code

5. Family Data: Father ☐ Living ☐ Deceased

Mother ☐ Living ☐ Deceased

Name _____

Address _____
(if different from applicant's)

Occupation _____

Current
Employer _____

Education (list college attended, if any, and degrees) _____

6. If you have a legal guardian other than the above, please name.

Name _____

Address _____

7. Number of brothers _____ Number of sisters _____ Number in college _____

5

8. Refer to the list of majors and codes on page 4, and indicate your preferred choice. Give the code for the major, as well as the name.

Code ☐☐☐   Name of Major _____

9. Have you previously applied for admission to Drexel? ☐ Yes ☐ No   If yes, when and what program? _____

10. Have you ever attended Drexel? ☐ Yes ☐ No   If yes, when? _____

11. Are you interested in a preprofessional program?

☐ 1. Pre-medicine   ☐ 2. Pre-dentistry   ☐ 3. Pre-veterinary medicine   ☐ 4. Pre-law   ☐ 5. Army ROTC

12. If admitted, you will ☐ Live at home (commuter)   ☐ Live at the University (resident)

13. Date of birth _____
        Month   Day   Year

14. The questions pertaining to sex and ethnic origin are optional and will be used for statistical purposes only.

Sex ☐ Male ☐ Female

Ethnic Origin ☐ 1. Caucasian ☐ 2. Black ☐ 4. American Indian ☐ 5. Asian or Pacific Islander ☐ 6. Hispanic ☐ 3. Other

15. Are you a citizen or legal permanent resident of the United States? ☐ Yes ☐ No

If you are not a U.S. citizen or a legal permanent resident, do you now hold a visa? ☐ Yes ☐ No

Type of visa (e.g. B-2, F-1, J-1, etc.) _____   Expiration date _____

If you are not a citizen or a legal permanent resident of the U.S., what is your country of citizenship? _____

16. Language spoken at home, if different from English _____

17. List relatives other than your parents who have attended or are attending Drexel.

_____ _____ _____
Name   Relationship   Curriculum   Degree-Year

_____ _____ _____
Name   Relationship   Curriculum   Degree-Year

_____ _____ _____
Name   Relationship   Curriculum   Degree-Year

18. Date(s) you have taken or plan to take College Board Scholastic Aptitude Test (SAT) (For all freshman students.) _____

TOEFL Test _____
(For those whose native language is not English.)

6

19. List below, in chronological order, the name of every high school, preparatory school, college, university, or other post-high school program which you have attended. All such institutions must be reported. You must request that the schools attended furnish the Office of Undergraduate Admissions with an official transcript.

Name of Institution	Location (city and state)	Dates (month and year) From	To

Present secondary school college code. (U.S. freshman applicants only. If you do not know, check with your college adviser.)

20. Please list any scholastic distinctions or honors you have won.

_____

_____

_____

21. List below in chronological order any employment or travel experiences you have had, including part-time work.

Work or Travel	Employer or Sponsor	Approximate Date	Hours per Week

22. List below your extracurricular activities and hobbies in the order of their importance to you. Check (✓) the left column beside those activities you hope to pursue at Drexel.

(✓)	Activity	Grade Participated (i.e., 9, 10, 11, 12)	Approximate Hours per Week	Positions Held or Honors Won

Only freshman applicants must respond to question 23. Please answer on a separate sheet of paper.

23. You will spend most of your years as a working professional in the 21st century. Describe the challenges you expect to face and explain how your college education should help you prepare to meet these challenges.

7

Only transfer applicants must respond to questions 24, 25, and 26.

24. Please list below the courses in which you are enrolled this term.

Course Title	Number of Credits

25. Have you participated in any special support services at your previous school, i.e., Act 101? (If so, you may qualify to participate in these services at Drexel.)   ☐ Yes   ☐ No

26. On a separate sheet of paper, please state your reasons for wanting to transfer to Drexel. If this is not your first change in colleges, please explain your reason for the previous transfer. An evaluation of your college education to date and reasons why your educational goals may be better served at Drexel should be included.

MUST BE READ BY ALL APPLICANTS:

It is our intent to get to know you as well as possible through this application. If you feel there is some information about yourself that has not been included and that we should know, please add it to this application.

Drexel University abides by the provisions of Public Law 93-380: Family Education Rights and Privacy Act, which grants the student the right to examine any admissions file which becomes a part of the student's permanent "education record." It is important to understand that "applicants for admissions" are not granted rights under this legislation. However, once an "applicant for admissions" becomes a "student" by enrolling and attending Drexel, any admissions file which becomes a part of the student's permanent "education record" becomes available to the student for review. Applicants should understand that only the transcript from the secondary school, College Board SAT and Achievement Test Score Reports and those portions of the application generated by the student will become part of the student's permanent "education record." Therefore, statements or evaluations provided by any individual as part of this application do not become part of the student's permanent "education record," and will not be available for the student's review.

I hereby certify that I have read and understand the above statement. I further certify that the information given by me on this application is complete and accurate.

_____

Date   Applicant's Signature

REQUEST FOR EARLY DECISION PROGRAM

To be completed by the Early Decision applicant: I have read and understand the description of the Early Decision Program as defined in this application. I will complete the required College Board Tests before December 1. If a positive decision is reached on this request, I understand that I will be notified of a decision by December 15. Drexel University is my first-choice college. I will accept a place in the September entering class if one is offered to me under the Early Decision Program, and I will withdraw all other applications at that time.

_____

Date   Applicant's Signature

To be completed by secondary school adviser for Early Decision candidates: I have discussed the request for Early Decision with this applicant and endorse him or her as a first choice for Drexel University. If the student is offered admission in December, I will remind him or her of the conditions of the above agreement.

_____

Signature   Position   Date

A report compiled by the University's Career Service Center summarizing recent graduates' responses to a survey of post-graduation plans is available upon request. For a copy of the report, call the admissions office at 215-895-2400, or write Drexel University, Office of Undergraduate Admissions, 32nd and Chestnut Streets, Philadelphia, Pa. 19104.

8

Drexel University
P H I L A D E L P H I A   P E N N S Y L V A N I A

TEACHER/COUNSELOR RECOMMENDATION

DESIRED STATUS (Please read the explanation of each status in the instructions before checking one.)

Freshman Admissions
☐ Early Decision Freshman for September 1991 *(Deadline November 15)*.
☐ Regular Decision Freshman for September 1991 *(Deadline March 1)*.
☐ Early Admission Freshman for September 1991 *(Deadline March 1)*.

Transfer Admissions
☐ Transfer Student for September 1991 *(Deadline August 15)*.
☐ Transfer Student for January 1992 *(Deadline November 15)*.
☐ Transfer Student for March 1992 *(Deadline February 15)*.
☐ Transfer Student for June 1992 *(Deadline May 15)*.

Student Name _____

Last   First   Middle

Social Security Number _____

Address _____

School _____

To the Applicant: After you have filled out the above, submit this form to a teacher or guidance counselor who has taught or advised you in the last two years. Transfer applicants should have a college faculty member fill out this form. It is particularly helpful if the teacher represents a subject area of continuing interest to you.

To the Teacher/Counselor: This student is applying for admission to Drexel University. We are interested in your candid appraisal of his/her intellectual motivation and the scholarly quality of his/her work. Your evaluation is very important to us and will be an integral element in our decision process.

This form should be returned to the following address by the deadline checked above by the student:

Director of Undergraduate Admissions
Drexel University
Philadelphia, Pa. 19104

Teacher/Counselor Name _____   Length of Acquaintance _____

Subject or Course _____   Dates Taught _____

Please comment on the quality and nature of the applicant's academic work.

How would you describe this student? Are there any personal strengths, weaknesses, or problems of which you feel we should be aware?

9

Compared to other college-bound students, check how you would rate this student in terms of academic skills and potential:

	No Basis	Below Average	Average	Good (above average)	Very Good (well above average)	Excellent (top 10%)	One of the Top Few Encountered in My Career
Creative, original thought							
Motivation							
Perseverance							
Independence, initiative							
Intellectual ability							
Academic achievement							
Written expression of ideas							
Effective class discussion							
Disciplined work habits							
Potential for growth							
SUMMARY EVALUATION							

Comments:

_____

_____

Signature_____

Date_____

10

Drexel University

P H I L A D E L P H I A   P E N N S Y L V A N I A

DEAN'S RECOMMENDATION FOR TRANSFER STUDENTS

DESIRED STATUS (Please read the explanation of each status in the instructions before checking one.)

☐ Transfer Student for September 1991 *(Deadline August 15)*.
☐ Transfer Student for January 1992 *(Deadline November 15)*.
☐ Transfer Student for March 1992 *(Deadline February 15)*.
☐ Transfer Student for June 1992 *(Deadline May 15)*.

To the Transfer Applicant: Please fill in the name of the college or university at which you are presently enrolled. Next, read the statement below, fill in the information requested and sign your name. Direct this form to the Dean of Student Affairs at the college or university in which you have been or are presently enrolled. The dean's office should complete the bottom portion of this form and return it to us at the address below.

University or College _____

I, the undersigned, authorize the release of the following information in support of my application for transfer to Drexel University. I understand that this information shall be completely confidential and shall not be disclosed to anyone, including the undersigned and his or her family, with the exception that the Director of Undergraduate Admissions may, in his or her sole discretion, disclose any part or all thereof to any person(s) in the employ of Drexel whom he or she deems advisable.

Applicant's Name (Print) _____   Social Security Number _____

Applicant's Signature _____   Date _____

To the Dean of Student Affairs: The above student either has been or is now enrolled at your institution. This student is now applying for admission to Drexel University. Please supply the information requested and then return this form to Drexel. If a reason for a change in your recommendation occurs after the deadline, we would appreciate hearing from you. Th s form should be returned to the following address by the deadline checked at the top of the form by the student.

Director of Undergraduate Admissions
Drexel University
Philadelphia, Pa. 19104

1. Is the above student currently enrolled at your college? _____

2. If not a current student, would he or she be permitted to re-enroll? _____

   If no, please explain _____

3. Has the student been under official censure by your college? _____

   If yes, please explain _____

4. Is the student recommended for transfer to Drexel? _____

   If not, please explain _____

11

5. How long have you known the student? _____   In what capacity? _____

6. Whom can we call for further information? _____

Telephone number _____

Signed _____   Position _____

Telephone Number _____   Date _____

Please use the space below for any comments or additional information which would be beneficial for evaluating the above student's application for admission, or which would facilitate his/her adjustment if accepted for admission to Drexel.

_____

_____

_____

_____

12

Source: Courtesy of Drexel University.

GLOSSARY

ABD "All but Degree" or "All but Dissertation": an informal title—not a degree—for someone who has completed all Ph.D. requirements except the dissertation

academic calendar important dates in an academic session

academic year in the United States, the period (roughly) September through June when schools, colleges, and universities are in full session

accreditation the formal approval of a department, college, or university teaching program by an outside agency, either regional or professional

add-drop a period just before or just after the beginning of an academic term when students may change their class schedules; also known as the adjustment period

adjunct faculty faculty members who teach part-time for a department without appointments in that department's regular faculty

admissions (1) the office that formally admits students to the university's programs; (2) the process of admitting students

Affidavit of Support (Form I-134) a government form completed by a sponsor who guarantees to support a student

American Council of Testing Program (ACT) a standard aptitude examination required of freshman applicants by many colleges and institutions

application the form on which a student requests admission to an educational institution

application fee a standard charge for processing an application for admission

approved housing list a list of apartments and other lodgings that have been approved by the educational institution for student rental

associate's degree a diploma conferred upon the successful completion of a two-year academic program; usually awarded by two-year colleges

B-2 visa the tourist visa—normally, not the proper visa for visitors to the United States who are also students

baccalaureate the bachelor's degree

bachelor's degree the diploma conferred by a college or university upon the successful completion of a four-year curriculum

bulletin see **catalog**

campus (1) the college or university grounds, usually characterized by park-like green spaces; (2) the grounds and buildings of a school, college, or university

catalog the educational institution's official statement of its courses, curricula, policies, etc., usually published annually; also called the bulletin

chancellor the chief executive of an educational institution, usually one with several campuses

class participation the student's contribution to class discussion, considered a valid criterion in grading

college (1) an institution organized to provide undergraduate education, either independently or as an administrative unit within a university; (2) a general term of reference to all post-secondary (tertiary) education

college fair an exposition or exhibition in which representatives of many educational institutions meet with interested applicants

college guide an annual publication, giving important information about most or all tertiary educational institutions

community college a two-year, post-secondary educational institution supported by the local community and offering curricula relevant to the community's needs

comprehensive examinations broad examinations covering material in several courses; typically, the examination at the end of a master's degree program

comprehensive school a secondary school that attempts to meet all of a community's educational needs, from vocational to college-preparatory

conditional admission acceptance into a college or university on condition that the applicant will meet the institution's minimum standard of English proficiency

consulate an overseas office of the U.S. government that issues visas to students and other travelers

cooperative education an educational program that requires work experience as well as classroom instruction

course outline the teacher's plan for the course, distributed to the students; also called the syllabus

credit (1) in general, the worth of a learning activity in fulfilling course or degree requirements; (2) specifically, a unit measuring the worth of a particular course, based upon the weekly number of hours the class spends in session

culture shock a state of homesickness, anger, or even illness resulting from the psychological discomfort of adjusting to a new culture

curriculum (pl.: **curricula**) the courses offered by an educational institution or the set of courses offered in a particular field by that educational institution

dean a professionally qualified, middle-level academic officer, usually one who supervises a college or post-baccalaureate school

dean's list a list, often published each term, of those students who have achieved a high grade-point average

development office the college or university office responsible for raising outside funds to support the institution's activities

dissertation the formal writing requirement—traditionally, an original contribution to knowledge—for an advanced degree, usually the Ph.D

distribution requirements (also, **general education requirements**) that part of general education that requires students to take a set number of courses in specified, varied subject areas

doctorate, doctoral degree the highest academic degree; e.g., the Ph.D. or Ed.D.

early admission the acceptance of a gifted student into college or university study before the student has finished the traditional twelve years of primary and secondary education

early decision early admission of a qualified student, usually based on the student's prior promise to accept the offer of admission

educational advising center an overseas office authorized to provide information about American educational institutions

ESL English as a Second Language, studied by nonnative speakers in an English-speaking country

F-1 visa the student visa for visitors studying in undergraduate, graduate, and English-language programs

faculty the body of full-time, permanent teachers in the department, the college, or the university

financial aid all forms of assistance provided by an institution to a student in order to meet the student's educational expenses

foreign student advisor the college or university administrator charged with meeting various needs of international faculty, staff, and students; often called the Director of International Services

freshman a first-year student in a four-year high school, or in a college or university

Fulbright award a government scholarship available to outstanding graduate students

funded research research efforts at an educational institution sponsored by agencies or companies outside that institution

general education requirements see **distribution requirements**

grade-point average the sum of the grade points earned in all courses taken by a student during the term divided by the number of credits the student has carried

grading policies a teacher's statement of the basis on which course grades will be calculated and awarded

graduate advisor the faculty member who serves as a general advisor to all graduate students in an academic department

graduate education post-baccalaureate (post-graduate) degree studies

Graduate Management Aptitude Test (GMAT) a standardized examination for applicants to graduate business programs

Graduate Record Examination (GRE) a set of standard examinations that determine readiness for graduate study

grants financial awards to educational institutions or individuals on the basis of scholastic ability or proposed research

high school secondary school, usually including grades 9–12 or 10–12

home stay a short-term or long-term visit of an international student in an American home

I-20 Form "Certificate of Eligibility for Nonimmigrant (F-1) Student Status," the document that authorizes the issuance of a student visa

I-94 Form the arrival-departure record, inserted into a visitor's passport

Immigration and Naturalization Service the U.S. government agency responsible for monitoring the status of all international visitors, including students

information letter a letter of application in which the student gives an educational institution sufficient information to determine his or her likely admissibility

institute of technology a tertiary institution whose principal curricula are in engineering fields

interactive classroom a class conducted so as to allow student participation in discussion, questions, answers, etc.

inter-library loan a service enabling students and faculty to borrow printed matter from another educational institution's library

international house a private residence hall that provides not only lodging but activities for international students and organizations

internationalization the encouragement, by an educational institution, of the admission of international students and the activities of international programs on its campus

international student orientation an event arranged at the beginning of an academic session for the purpose of helping international students settle in to their new environment

J-1 visa the exchange visitor visa, usually given to international faculty members or government-sponsored students

jet lag a state of disorientation caused by airplane travel across several time zones in a few hours

junior a third-year student in a four-year high school, or in a college or university

junior high school lower education grades 7–9 (occasionally grades 6–8), gathered into a separate administrative unit between primary school and high school

K–12 kindergarten through 12th grade, the total of primary and secondary education

Law School Admissions Test (LSAT) the standard examination for applicants to law schools throughout the United States

lease the housing contract between a landlord and a tenant

liberal arts the humanities, broadly considered; the traditional, nontechnical subjects

M-1 visa the visa issued to students enrolling in trade and vocational schools

major (1) a student's field of study; the specialized component in his or her curriculum; (2) the student himself or herself, as in "She's a psychology major."

master's degree an earned, post-baccalaureate degree, usually requiring one to two years of study

meal plan a student's contract with an educational institution for regular meal service

Medical College Admissions Test (MCAT) the standard test for applicants to medical schools throughout the United States

minor limited but specialized learning in a second field; see **major**

multiple-choice test an objective examination giving the student several choices of answers to a question, of which one answer is correct

multiple measurements the practice of measuring a student's achievements or accomplishments via several means, and not just by examinations

nationality associations student groups each made up of students from one country

office hours established hours during which the instructor will be in his or her office to consult with students

on-campus employment authorized student employment by college or university offices and departments

participation see **class participation**

plagiarism the serious offense of using the words or ideas of another person and pretending they are one's own

pre-application form a form by which an educational institution screens a student's potential for admission

preschool school-like activities preceding kindergarten

probation a status imposed on students who are doing unsatisfactory work, and maintained until they either achieve a satisfactory grade-point average or are dropped from the university or from the degree program

professor the common honorific for all university faculty members who are ranked as assistant, associate, or (full) professors

provost a vice-president and the chief academic officer who supervises the academic policies and budgets of a college or university

qualifying examination an examination that tests a students' qualifications for doctoral work

quarter system the academic calendar in which the year is divided into four sessions, each with approximately ten weeks of instruction

rankings the attempt to rate academic institutions in some order of excellence

recitation (section) a session for a small group of students attending a large lecture course; here the students review assignments, discuss homework, etc.

recruiting agent a person who, for a fee, attempts to provide international applicants in the recruiting agent's country with access to American education

referees those who write letters of reference in support of student applicants

registration the formal process, conducted term by term, of enrolling students in coursework

research assistantship an award made to a graduate student in return for assistance with departmental research

residence halls supervised student dormitories

residency requirement an educational institution's requirement of a minimum number of courses/credits that must be completed on its campus

resident assistant a student employed by a residence hall to help in various activities and provide general supervision

rolling admissions the process of acting upon admissions applications as they arrive, rather than all at once in a set time period

scholarship (1) the practice of producing scholarly work; (2) a grant of money to a student, awarded (usually) on the basis of academic performance

Scholastic Aptitude Test (SAT) a standardized external examination of mathematical and verbal skills, taken by high school students to demonstrate their qualifications for college work

section one offering of a course that is offered at several times and places in the same term

semester system the most common academic calendar, consisting of two terms of approximately fifteen weeks of instruction

senior a fourth-year student in a four-year high school or in a college or university

Social Security number a governmentally assigned number usually needed for identification purposes for employment and in banks, educational institutions, etc.

sophomore a second-year student in a four-year high school or in a college or university

Speaking Proficiency English Assessment Kit (SPEAK) see **Test of Spoken English**

sponsor a person or organization agreeing to meet a student's educational expenses

student health clinic an on-campus clinic providing initial treatment and referral for injured or sick students

Student Life the division of a college or university that promotes student activities and well-being; sometimes called "Student Affairs" or "Student Services"

Supplement Data Sheet (Form OF-156) a form used in screening student applicants in U.S. consulates

syllabus a teacher's plan for a course, distributed to the students; also called the course outline

teaching assistant a graduate student who, while pursuing an advanced degree, is employed part-time by the university to carry out departmental teaching, or teaching-related duties; often called a "TA"

tenure the status of a permanent member of the faculty, awarded on the basis of scholarship, teaching, or service

tertiary institution a college, university, or institute of technology offering post-secondary education

testing centers designated offices in the United States and overseas that administer various aptitude and proficiency examinations

Test of English as a Foreign Language (TOEFL) the standard test of an international applicant's English ability

Test of Spoken English (TSE) an oral examination administered overseas to determine an applicant's fluency in English; recycled versions of the test administered in the United States are known as "Speaking Proficiency English Assessment Kit," or SPEAK

Test of Written English (TWE) a standard measure of writing ability in which the applicant is asked to compose an essay on a set topic

textbook a book required for a course and providing a systematic presentation of course material

transcript an educational institution's formal record of a student's academic work and other significant accomplishments

transfer credits credits awarded toward the degree on the basis of studies at another institution; also called advance(d) credits

transfer evaluation the award of credits given by an educational institution to a student for work he or she has completed at another institution

transfer student a student (usually, undergraduate) who changes enrollment from one educational institution to another

trimester system an academic calendar in which the year is divided into three terms

tuition the amount of money charged by an educational institution for taking classes

United States Information Agency/Service (USIA/USIS) a U.S. agency whose overseas offices are responsible for providing information about American life, education, and other matters

university an institution of higher education consisting of several colleges that award graduate degrees and engage in research activities

visa authorization, via a passport stamp, by a consulate to visit or study in the country represented by the consulate

"whole person" the term summarizing the belief that education should help students develop skills, physical abilities, and social awareness as well as specialized knowledge

BIBLIOGRAPHY

Accredited Institutions of Postsecondary Education. Washington: American Council on Education, 1989.

"America's Best Colleges." *U.S. News & World Report*. Publ. annually.

Barnes, Gregory A. *The American University: A World Guide*. Philadelphia: ISI Press, 1984.

Bibliography for Educational Advising Centers. Washington: Action Document, 1989.

The Chronicle of Higher Education. Publ. weekly, 48 times per year.

The College Cost Book, 1989–90. New York: College Entrance Examination Board, 1989.

The College Handbook: Foreign Student Supplement. New York: College Entrance Examination Board, 1989.

Directory of Overseas Educational Advising Centers (1989–90). New York: College Entrance Examination Board, 1989.

Donner, Michael. *How to Beat the S.A.T. and All Standardized Multiple-Choice Tests*. New York: Workman, 1981.

Eckland, Bruce K. "College Entrance Examination Trends." *The Rise and Fall of National Test Scores*. Gilbert R. Austin and Herbert Garber, eds. New York: Academic Press, 1982.

Ehret, Charles F., and Lynne Waller Scanlon. *Overcoming Jet Lag*. New York: Berkley, 1983.

English Language and Orientation Programs. New York: Institute of International Education, publ. annually.

Entering Higher Education in the United States. New York: College Entrance Examination Board, 1989.

Feder, Bernard. *The Complete Guide to Taking Tests.* Englewood Cliffs, NJ: Prentice-Hall, 1979.

Gourman, J. *The Gourman Report: A Rating of Graduate and Professional Programs in American and International Universities.* Los Angeles: National Education Standards; publ. annually.

Graduate School and You: A Guide for Prospective Graduate Students. Washington: Council of Graduate Schools, 1989.

GRE Information Bulletin. Princeton, NJ: Educational Testing Service, 1990.

A Guide to the Admission of Foreign Students. Washington: National Association for Foreign Student Affairs, no date.

Guidelines for the Use of GRE Scores. Princeton, NJ: Educational Testing Service, 1989.

Hemp-Lyons, Liz. *Preparing for the Test of Written English.* New York: Newbury House, 1989.

If You Want to Study in the United States. 6 booklets. Washington: United States Information Agency, 1986.

NAFSA Principles for International Educational Exchange. Washington: National Association for Foreign Student Affairs, 1983.

National Center for Education Statistics. *The Condition of Education, 1989.* 3 vols. Washington: U.S. Department of Education, 1989.

Smith, Eugene H., and Gary Althen. Adviser's Manual of Federal Regulations Affecting Foreign Students and Scholars. Washington: National Association of Foreign Student Affairs, 1989.

Taking the SAT. New York: College Entrance Examination Board, 1989.

Zikopoulos, Marianthi, ed. *Open Doors 1989/90: Report on International Educational Exchange.* New York: Institute for International Education, 1990.

INDEX

Living expenses, 87
  as criteria in choosing schools,
    41–42
Loans, 89
Lodging on arrival, 116

M

M-1 visa, 100, 110
Maintenance, 24
Master's program, 161–62
Medical College Admissions Test
  (MCAT), 60
Medical insurance, 117–18
Mentor, professor as, 157–58
Middle school, 17
Move, planning your, 113–22
Multiculturalism, 12
Multiple-choice test format, 54
Multiple measurements, 145–47

N

National Liaison Committee on
  Foreign Student Admissions, 72
Non-need scholarships, 90

O

Office hours, 144
On-campus, term of, 22
On-campus employment, 92, 95
Orientation, for international student,
  134–35
Overcoming Jet Lag, 127

P

Packing, 124–25
Passport, 105
Personal funds, 88
Plagiarism, 148, 164–65
Planning of trip, 119–20
Population density, as criteria in
  choosing school, 39–41
*Preparing for the Test of Written
  English,* 56
Preschool, 17
President, 23
Primary school, 17
Private institutions, 20
Private schools, 17
Professor, 26
  as mentor, 157–58

Public institutions, 20
Public schools, 17, 18
Punctuality, 135–36

Q

Quarters, 74

R

Rankings, 45–46
Recitation sections, 143
Recruiting agents, 51–53
Recruitment of international students,
  9–10
Reference books, 177
Registration for classes, 132
Requirements
  academic credit system, 29–30
  distribution requirements, 28–29
Research assistants (RA), 12, 97–98
Research, 154–55
  availability of funding, 48, 154–55
Residence halls, living in, 42, 114–16
Residency requirement, 79
Resident assistants (RA), 114
Reverse chronological order, 77
Reverse culture shock, 136
Rolling admissions, 80

S

Scholarships, 89
  sources for, 92
Scholastic Aptitude Test (SAT), 57–58
  prep courses, 58
School(s). *See also* College(s);
  Universities
  academic considerations, 44–45
  choosing right, 32–50
  climate and physical environment,
    42
  criteria in choosing
    institutional size, 37–38
    population density, 39–41
  educational and living expenses,
    41–42
  housing accommodations, 42
  rankings, 45–46
School board, 17
Secondary school class rank,
  importance of, 57
Senior high school, 17

If you would like to make suggestions for this book
and get his advice, you may write Dr. Barnes at:
  The English Language Center
  Drexel University
  Philadelphia, PA 19104
  USA